HERALDRY
of the World

Written and illustrated by
Carl Alexander von Volborth, K.St.J., A.I.H.

Edited by
D. H. B. Chesshyre, M.A., F.S.A., Rouge Croix Pursuivant

BLANDFORD PRESS
POOLE   DORSET

First published in the U.K. 1973
Reprinted 1979

English text © 1973 Blandford Press Ltd,
Link House, West Street, Poole, Dorset BH15 1LL

ISBN 0 7137 0647 3

Originally published in Denmark as
Alverdens Heraldik i Farver.

World Copyright © Politikens Forlag A/S
Copenhagen, Denmark

Translated into English by
Bob and Inge Gosney

Colour sheets printed in Denmark by F. E. Bording A/S
Filmset in Baskerville and Univers by Cranmer Brown (Filmsetters) Ltd and bound by
Richard Clay (The Chaucer Press) Ltd, Bungay, Suffolk
Printed in Great Britain by
Fletcher & Son Ltd, Norwich

CONTENTS

Text

EDITOR'S PREFACE

This useful little book was written originally in America by Carl Alexander von Volborth and has subsequently appeared in Germany and Denmark, the Danish edition having been extensively adapted and edited by Sven Tito Achen and published by Politikens Forlag in 1972.

The present edition is a translation from the Danish, and the English editor has been at pains to preserve the text of the Danish edition, merely making minor amendments where necessary for the benefit of the English and American reader and endeavouring to ensure that the sections relating to English heraldry are in keeping with current heraldic practice as observed at the College of Arms. He does not claim to vouch for the accuracy of every detail, as the work covers a very wide spectrum, but he feels confident that the book will fill an important gap in the literature of heraldry.

D. H. B. Chesshyre   London, 1973.

THE ORIGINS OF HERALDRY

It was during the early decades of the twelfth century, between the First and Second Crusades, that nobles, knights and princes began to identify themselves and their equipment, their shields in particular, by the use of simple figures in clear, contrasting colours, and this must be considered the origin of what is now called heraldry. For warriors to decorate themselves and their shields was certainly nothing new; it had been a feature of almost all ages and cultures (see p. 9), in Europe as well as elsewhere, since long before the twelfth century. The particular characteristic of these new shield devices was the fact that they remained more or less the same for each individual and then gradually became hereditary; that their use was extended to practically all classes and institutions in the community; and that this developed into a detailed and permanent system for the elaboration and application of the insignia within a short time.

The earliest arms were adopted at will by the individual, but from about 1400 onwards sovereigns began to grant insignia by means of letters patent, often, but by no means always, as the prerogative of the nobility. Families whose nobility originates in such letters patent or in similar elevations or creations are said to hold patents of nobility; the older aristocracy, whose origins are lost in the darkness of the Middle Ages, is known as the 'old nobility'. But concurrently with the granting of insignia by letters patent, people continued to assume insignia for themselves and, provided that devices were used that were not already the prerogative of others nor resembled another bearing too closely, this was tolerated, at least in the Middle Ages in most European countries.

From the warrior class the practice spread to the Church, to burghers and farmers, and to municipal governments, craft guilds and other institutions. Almost from the beginning of heraldry women too had the right to bear arms. (See also pp. 42–4.)

The coat of arms above belonged to Archduke Maximilian of Austria who became King of the Romans in 1486 and, as Maximilian I, Emperor 1493–1519. The two halves of the inescutcheon stand for Austria and Burgundy.

HERALDIC CHARGES

1. Arms of San Marino.

2. Arms of Andorra.

3. Arms of Liechtenstein.

4. Arms of Luxembourg.

5. Arms of Monaco.

What were the origins of these new devices?

For the warrior class there were three main sources of inspiration: the banners and standards that already existed in the pre-heraldic period, the purely functional plating or reinforcement given to the shield – nails, ridges, strips, crosses, etc. – and finally what might be called totemic signs: figures, often of animals or fabulous beasts, expressing chivalrous ideals, such as warlike lions, eagles, falcons, unicorns, and so on.

For princes and the Church many devices were probably derived from seals, the use of which antedates heraldry proper, or from religious symbols. It was also natural for people of various stations to choose devices relevant to their profession or way of life. The bishop included a crosier in his escutcheon, the priest a chalice, the squire a spur, the brewer a barrel, the smith a hammer, the fisherman a fish trap, and so on.

A large number of these were what are called 'canting arms', i.e. they illustrate or refer to the bearer's name, for example a falcon for the name Falconer, or *hirondelles* – swallows – for Arundel. Further reference will be made to this on p. 34. It must also be mentioned that many arms were adaptations or imitations of existing coats.

The word 'heraldry' is derived from the word 'herald'. The herald of the Middle Ages was a messenger between rulers, a sort of ambassador, and he gradually became responsible for the organising of state ceremonies and tournaments. Particularly in the case of tournaments it was of the greatest importance for him to be able to recognise the devices of the participants, and thus the herald became so expert in 'armory' that it was eventually named after him. Heralds attempted to work out registers in order to keep control of all the arms in use within their official sphere.

In Great Britain heralds have survived until the present day and still exercise a certain authority. In England this is invested in the College of Arms (the Corporation of Kings, Heralds and Pursuivants of Arms) and, in Scotland, in the Office of Lord Lyon King of Arms. In other countries too there are offices which deal with heraldic problems, particularly those of state and local government. This is true of Denmark, Sweden, Finland, Holland, Belgium, Spain, Ireland and South Africa. Most of these however are of more recent origin.

PRE-HERALDRY

Pre-heraldic shield devices and head-dresses etc.

6. Roman officer about A.D. 1.

7. Assyrian warrior c. 800 B.C.

11. Eagle standard of the Roman legions; the eagle reappears in 12.

12. Eagle in the arms of the Holy Roman Empire, fourteenth century.

8. Noble Inca warrior, Peru, sixteenth century.

9. Sioux brave, North America, nineteenth century.

10. Masai warrior, East Africa, c. 1900.

NEW USAGES AND FORMS

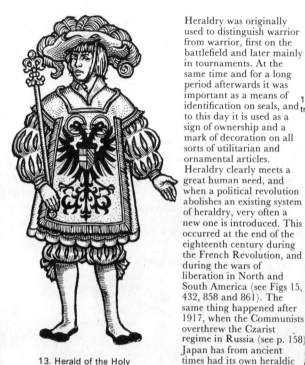

13. Herald of the Holy Roman Empire, sixteenth century.

Heraldry was originally used to distinguish warrior from warrior, first on the battlefield and later mainly in tournaments. At the same time and for a long period afterwards it was important as a means of identification on seals, and to this day it is used as a sign of ownership and a mark of decoration on all sorts of utilitarian and ornamental articles. Heraldry clearly meets a great human need, and when a political revolution abolishes an existing system of heraldry, very often a new one is introduced. This occurred at the end of the eighteenth century during the French Revolution, and during the wars of liberation in North and South America (see Figs 15, 432, 858 and 861). The same thing happened after 1917, when the Communists overthrew the Czarist regime in Russia (see p. 158). Japan has from ancient times had its own heraldic system which is in some respects reminiscent of the European.

14. Arms of Finland, traditional.

15. Emblem of Guatemala, revolutionary.

16. Emblem of Communist China.

17. Emblem of the Emperor of Japan.

18. Arms of Switzerland, traditional.

19. Arms of Turkey, adapted from the traditional.

20. Arms of Israel, almost traditional.

SHIELD AND HELMET

21. Armorial bearings of the German Nobel prizewinner, Dr Emil von Behring (1854–1917).

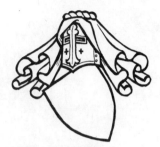

22. Early pattern for Esquire or Gentleman and *Uradel (noblesse de race)*.

23. Later pattern for Esquire or Gentleman and *Bürger*, sometimes also used by nobility.

The principal component of a coat of arms is the shield, sometimes called the escutcheon, decorated with one or more devices or 'charges'; to this is added the helmet with mantling and crest.

According to the bearer's rank, the fashion of the age or individual preference, there can be added coronets or other insignia of rank, insignia of office, supporters, mantling, badges, a scroll with motto, etc. All these details and others will be discussed in the following pages.

24. Pattern for nobility since the Renaissance.

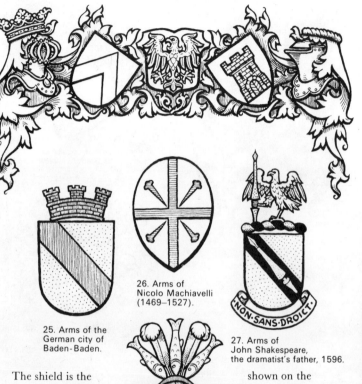

25. Arms of the German city of Baden-Baden.

26. Arms of Nicolo Machiavelli (1469–1527).

27. Arms of John Shakespeare, the dramatist's father, 1596.

The shield is the most important part of a coat of arms. It can take practically any form, depending on period, place, function, situation or the whim of the heraldic artist. Examples are shown on the following pages. A shield can be used on its own (Fig. 26), with a crown above (Fig. 25), with helmet and crest (Fig. 28), or with crest alone, without helmet (Fig. 27).

28. Arms of the German baronial family of von Braun, of which the rocket expert Wernher von Braun was a member.

SHIELD AND HELMET

13th century

13th century

13th century

Italy, 14th century

29. Anglo-Saxon warrior, eleventh century.

30. A shield with curved notch cut away in dexter chief (originally for the lance) is called *à bouche*.

31. Norman warrior, eleventh century.

France, 15th century

Italy, 15th century

Burgundy, 14th century

Germany, 14th century

32. Coat of arms in the baroque style, seventeenth century.

SHIELD AND HELMET

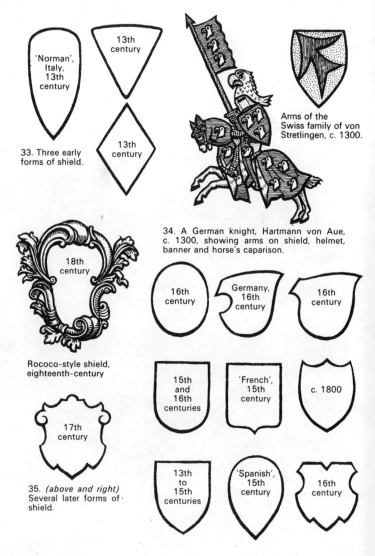

'Norman', Italy, 13th century

13th century

13th century

33. Three early forms of shield.

Arms of the Swiss family of von Stretlingen, c. 1300.

34. A German knight, Hartmann von Aue, c. 1300, showing arms on shield, helmet, banner and horse's caparison.

18th century

Rococo-style shield, eighteenth-century

16th century

Germany, 16th century

16th century

15th and 16th centuries

'French', 15th century

c. 1800

17th century

35. *(above and right)* Several later forms of shield.

13th to 15th centuries

'Spanish', 15th century

16th century

POT HELM AND GREAT HELM

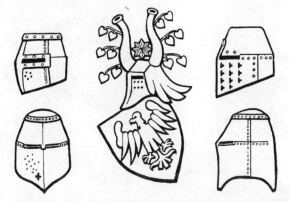

36. The earliest form of helmet used in heraldry, going back to the thirteenth century, was the pot helm which usually had a flat top. Around 1300 it was gradually replaced by the great helm which had a conical top and rested on the warrior's shoulders. With this helmet the crest came into general use. From the end of the fourteenth century it began to be replaced by the tilting helm (see next page). In Scotland the great helm is used by gentlemen and esquires regardless of the antiquity of the arms, but in most other countries it is generally used only with arms which can be traced back to the thirteenth or fourteenth centuries.

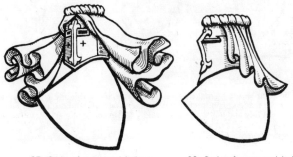

37. Style of arms and helmet for ancient German nobility.

38. Style of arms and helmet for Scottish esquire and gentleman.

TOURNAMENT HELMET
(OR JOUSTING HELMET)

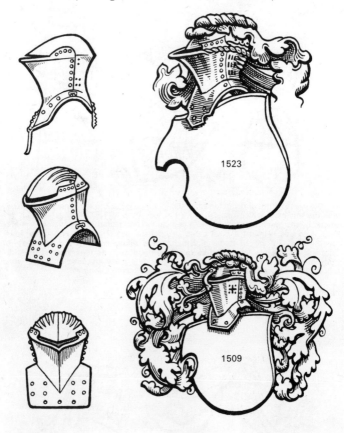

39. The tournament helmet derives its name from the tourney or tournament, i.e. fighting with lances as a form of sport. It came into use about the beginning of the fifteenth century and it was used in heraldry for several centuries, in non-aristocratic arms especially.

HELMET AND MANTLING

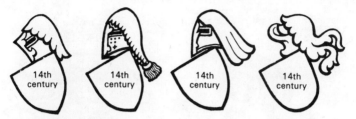

40. Mantling was originally a piece of material fastened to the top of the helmet and hanging down over the warrior's neck and shoulders, possibly to protect him from the heat of the sun.

41. It was probably in connection with the fashion of the times (see below) that heraldic mantling was developed during the fifteenth century as flowing drapery with pleats and creases, scallops and slashing. The tinctures of the mantling are as a rule the same as those of the shield, the most important colour being on the outside and the most important 'metal' on the inside, though there are many exceptions.

During the sixteenth century and later it developed into what is sometimes regarded as foliage (see p. 16).

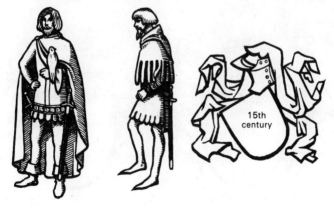

17

THE BARRED HELMET
(OR BARRED BURGONET)

1520

42. The barred helmet came into use in the course of the fifteenth century. It is not certain whether it was actually worn during the tournaments or whether it was merely a parade helmet decorated with the appropriate crests, displayed by the participants before the contest.

In the course of the Renaissance and at later periods attempts were made to ensure that the use of the barred helmet in a coat of arms was reserved for the nobility, but this was not entirely successful (see text p. 103). In the seventeenth century and later several countries tried to establish the rule that the position of the helmet (profile or *en face*) and the number of bars should indicate the various ranks, but this classification was difficult to enforce.

1526

1526

THE VISORED HELMET
(OR ARMET)

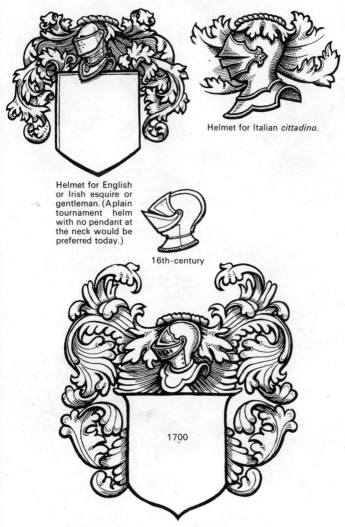

Helmet for Italian *cittadino*.

Helmet for English or Irish esquire or gentleman. (A plain tournament helm with no pendant at the neck would be preferred today.)

16th-century

1700

43. Helmet with visor as used in Italy, England and Ireland.

THE VISORED HELMET
(OR ARMET)

45 and 46. From the sixteenth century onwards helmets with open visors, usually affronty and at times in gold, were used by kings and princes (see Fig. 440).

44. Tournament helm, 1526.

49. After the Renaissance, when heraldry no longer had any practical function and had become merely 'paper' heraldry, many errors and absurdities arose. Below can be seen a Spanish example of this: the mantling is not attached to the top of the helmet, but to its inside. The combination of visor and bars on the helmet does seem actually to have been used, however.

47. Helmet for Italian patrician.

48. Helmet for British knight or baronet, steel-coloured.

HELMET AND ROBE OF ESTATE

50. In the seventeenth and eighteenth centuries another form of mantling came into prominence, as shown in the design for a coat of arms, *right*. This is the 'robe of estate', represented in some countries in the bunched manner illustrated here which resembles the tent-like 'pavilion' used by many hereditary sovereigns (see Figs 275 and 276–80).

51. The small Spanish mantle, or *mantelete,* which in the illustration on the left is red and lined with ermine, seems to be a transitional stage between mantling and robe of estate, although very early examples of mantling in capeline form may be found (see Fig. 206).

52. Arms of the Swedish botanist Carolus Linnaeus (Carl von Linné) (1707–78), ennobled in 1757. The robe of estate was very popular as a form of mantling with the new nobility of eighteenth-century Sweden.

MORE THAN ONE HELMET

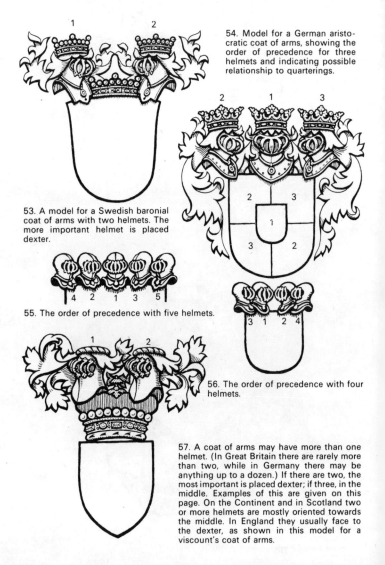

54. Model for a German aristocratic coat of arms, showing the order of precedence for three helmets and indicating possible relationship to quarterings.

53. A model for a Swedish baronial coat of arms with two helmets. The more important helmet is placed dexter.

55. The order of precedence with five helmets.

56. The order of precedence with four helmets.

57. A coat of arms may have more than one helmet. (In Great Britain there are rarely more than two, while in Germany there may be anything up to a dozen.) If there are two, the most important is placed dexter; if three, in the middle. Examples of this are given on this page. On the Continent and in Scotland two or more helmets are mostly oriented towards the middle. In England they usually face to the dexter, as shown in this model for a viscount's coat of arms.

TINCTURES

SINISTER
DEXTER

58. The shield is described as seen by the bearer standing behind it. Thus the heraldic right and the heraldic left are the opposite of the normal right and left, and this can be confusing. It is therefore preferable to use the international terms 'dexter' and 'sinister'.

59. Counterchanging: a shield divided vertically (per pale) into red and white with a rose counterchanged.

60. Counterchanging: a coat divided horizontally (per fess) the two stars counterchanged.

| Or (yellow or gold) | Argent (white or silver) | Azure (blue) | Gules (red) | Vert (green) | Purpure (purple) |

| Sable (black) | Sable (black) | Ermine | Ermines | Vair | Counter vair |

63. Vair, older form.

61 and 62. *(above)* Gold and silver are called metals and blue, red, green, purple and black are called colours. Ermine and vair are called furs. In good heraldry colour must not be superimposed on colour nor metal on metal, but metal and colour should alternate. The system of indicating the tinctures with the aid of shading (or hatching) was developed in

64. Another variation of vair.

the seventeenth century. There are however other systems than the one shown here, so care is necessary when interpreting early blazons.

DIVISIONS AND ORDINARIES

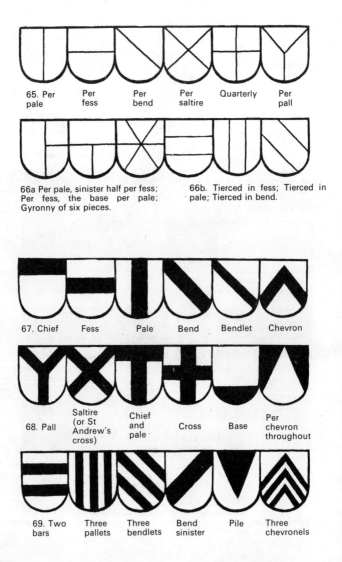

65. Per pale   Per fess   Per bend   Per saltire   Quarterly   Per pall

66a Per pale, sinister half per fess; Per fess, the base per pale; Gyronny of six pieces.

66b. Tierced in fess; Tierced in pale; Tierced in bend.

67. Chief   Fess   Pale   Bend   Bendlet   Chevron

68. Pall   Saltire (or St Andrew's cross)   Chief and pale   Cross   Base   Per chevron throughout

69. Two bars   Three pallets   Three bendlets   Bend sinister   Pile   Three chevronels

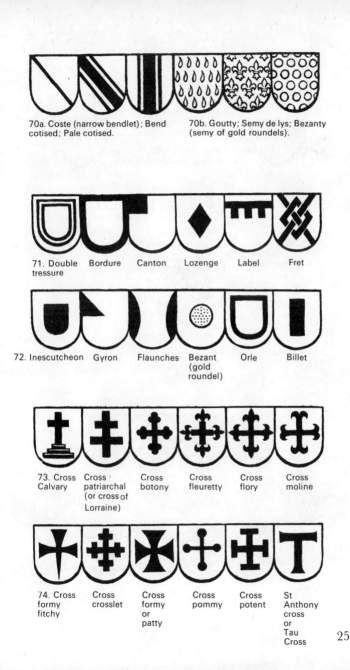

70a. Coste (narrow bendlet); Bend cotised; Pale cotised.

70b. Goutty; Semy de lys; Bezanty (semy of gold roundels).

71. Double tressure — Bordure — Canton — Lozenge — Label — Fret

72. Inescutcheon — Gyron — Flaunches — Bezant (gold roundel) — Orle — Billet

73. Cross Calvary — Cross patriarchal (or cross of Lorraine) — Cross botony — Cross fleuretty — Cross flory — Cross moline

74. Cross formy fitchy — Cross crosslet — Cross formy or patty — Cross pommy — Cross potent — St Anthony cross or Tau Cross

PARTITION AND BORDER LINES

Engrailed

Invected

Indented

75a. Fess engrailed.

75b. Fess invected (or invecked).

Dancetty

Dancetty floretty

Wavy or Undy

Embattled

Nebuly

Raguly

Dovetailed

Potent

76. These forms can be used for border lines as well as for divisional lines as in the example above.

Embattled grady (or battled, embattled)

Urdy

Rayonny

77. A field can be partitioned in many ways. For these four examples see the terms on p. 184

78. Decorative treatment of the surface of a shield is called diaper.

80. Other methods of dividing the field. See p. 184

79. Another example of diaper (see Fig. 78).

CHARGES

Almost anything can be used as a heraldic charge but the depiction is as a rule greatly simplified or stylised.

81. Eagle close.

82. Lion sejant.

83. Eagle displayed.

84. Lion passant.

85. Lion couchant.

86. Eagle rising or volant.

87. Lion rampant.

88. Lion salient. 89. Lion statant reguardant.

90. Lion dormant.

CHARGES

91. Lion rampant reguardant.

92. Double-headed eagle.

93. Lion rampant guardant.

94. Lion sejant erect.

95. Lion sejant affronty.

96. Lion rampant queue fourchy.

97. Fish hauriant.

98. Lion rampant double-headed and coward.

99. Lion sejant erect guardant.

100. Fish urinant.

101. Dolphin.

102. Fish naiant

103. Fish naiant.

104. Dolphin embowed.

105. Escallop.

CHARGES

106. Demi-goat with collar (as a crest).

107. Bull rampant to the sinister.

108. Demi-ram issuant from a coronet (as a crest).

109. Lion's face (often blazoned as a leopard's face).

110. Pelican in its nest feeding its young ('in its piety').

111. Wolf's head erased.

112. Horse rampant.

113. Paschal Lamb.

114. A crane with a stone in its claw ('in its vigilance').

115. Talbot's head issuant from a coronet.

116. Saracen's face wreathed about the temples.

117. Cock.

118. Clenched fist.

119. Martlet.

120. Vambraced arm with coronet scimitar.

CHARGES

121. Boar's head couped at the neck.

122. Lymphad.

123. Boar's head couped close.

124. Swan rousant.

125. Quatrefoil.

126. Castle.

127. Cinquefoil.

128. Hart.

129. Trefoil.

130. Lime-tree issuant from base.

131. Tower.

132. Oak-tree eradicated.

133. Fleur-de-lys.

134. Rod of Aesculapius.

135. Rose.

136. Rod of Mercury or caduceus.

137. Antlers or attires. (In Scotland, 'tynes'.)

CHARGES

138. Horseshoe.

139. Battle axe.

140. Scimitar.

141. Arrow.

142. Anchor.

143. Wings conjoined.

144. Escarbuncle..

145. Sword.

146. Hunting horn.

147. Buffalo horns.

148. Sun in splendour.

149. Moon decrescent.

150. Crescent.

151. Caltrap.

152. Moon increscent.

153. Moon increscent with face.

154. Five-pointed mullet.

155. Millrind.

156. Chessrook.

157. Clarion.

158. Covered cup.

159. Pheon.

160. Maunche.

161. Estoile.

162. Water-bouget.

CHARGES: FABULOUS CREATURES

163. Wyvern.

164. Double-tailed mermaid, also called melusine.

165. Heraldic tiger. Occurs particularly in English heraldry.

166. Dragon.

167. Mermaid, often depicted with comb and glass.

168. Heraldic antelope (usually shown with horns serrated). Occurs particularly in English heraldr

169. Pegasus.

170. Griffin.

171. Unicorn.

CHARGES: FABULOUS CREATURES

172. Sea-horse.

173. Harpy displayed.

174. Heraldic sea-lion.

175. Type of heraldic panther.

176. Cockatrice.

177. Griffin in the Russian city of Sebastopol's coat of arms.

179. Cherub's face.

178. Crowned basilisk or wyvern in the arms of the city of Kazan in Russia (see Fig. 808).

181. Seraph's face.

180. Crowned heraldic panther in the arms of the city of Graz in Austria.

182. Crowned griffin's head in the city arms of Malmö.

CANTING ARMS

Canting arms are arms in which the charge or charges illustrate the holder's name or, by a stretch of the imagination, his way of life or even his address. As stated on p. 8 there are a tremendous number of canting arms, certainly far more than we realise, because many of them may be a play upon the meaning or pronunciation of a name no longer used or long since forgotten.

Canting arms have been popular from the very beginnings of heraldry, among all classes of the community, from the castle in the arms of the King of Castile (see Fig. 271) to the arms of craftsmen and farmers. From the thirteenth and fourteenth centuries we even have examples of noble families rejecting their old, non-canting arms in favour of new, canting ones. One example is that of the German counts, later princes, von Henneberg. They exchanged a wall and an eagle for a hen (German: *Henne*). The Danish–Swedish noble family of Trolle originally bore a coat of arms tierced, but changed over to a troll (a supernatural giant or dwarf).

On the next page are examples of German and English canting arms, and the rest of the book contains many others: from Germany, Bach (a beck) (Fig. 557) and Dürer (a door, German: *Tür*) (Fig. 562); from Austria, Rothschild (Fig. 580); from Switzerland, Uri (aurochs) (Fig. 597); from Italy, Turin (a bull, Latin: *taurus*) (Fig. 708); from Norway, Bull (Fig. 751); from Sweden, Goos (a goose) (Fig. 780); and from Finland, Horn (Fig. 786). But canting arms are not always so easy to decipher. They may be based on a dialect, or even on a foreign language. There is the example of the Danish vicar, Lauritz Petersen, who in the seventeenth century latinised his name to Petraeus and, as this was related to the Greek word *petra*, meaning a rock, he went one step further and translated it into Syrian (*Thura*). Since there is a Latin word of a similar sound which means incense the Thura family included a censer in their coat of arms. This is an example of a punning charge. But the surname could also be chosen to refer to the charge, and this often explains the meaning of the bearings. The Danish nobility were in 1526 compelled to adopt permanent surnames and quite a number of families took their name from their escutcheons, like the families of Rosenkrantz (the wreath of roses surmounting the helmet, see Fig. 729) and Gyldenstjerne (a gold star).

There are also many non-aristocratic families whose arms originated in the name of the family house and where the charge eventually became the family name.

There were also instances where the charge and the name were created simultaneously, such as Tordenskjold (meaning literally 'thunder shield') and his thunderbolt, see Fig. 743.

CANTING ARMS

183. Von Baum. *Baum*=tree.

184. Von Radecke. *Rad*=wheel, *Ecke*=corner.

185. Von Hahn. *Hahn*=cock.

186. Von Rappard. *Rappe*=black horse.

187. Von Brunn. *Brunnen*= well.

188. Von Merkatz. *Meerkatze*= monkey.

189. City arms of Ahlen. *Aal*=eel.

190. Von Specht. *Specht*=woodpecker.

191. City arms of Bibra. *Biber* =beaver.

193. City arms of Göttingen (a capital G).

192. City arms of Louvain or Löwen. *Löwe* =lion.

194. The Horners' Company, London, includes three hunting horns in its arms.

195. The Barbers' Company, London, included three fleams for blood-letting in its arms.

35

CRESTS

The fashion of placing a wreath, made up of two twisted bands of silk, designed to keep the mantling firmly attached to the helmet, was started in about the middle of the fourteenth century. The wreath (or 'torse') was also used as a support for the crest (see the following pages) and to hide the join between helmet and crest.

A crown was often used for the same purpose. These crowns or coronets were originally the privilege of noble families, but later they were used by other classes and are therefore not necessarily a sign of rank.

As well as the traditional crest-coronet (see Figs. 205, 208 and 209), various other forms of crown gradually came into being, examples of which are shown below.

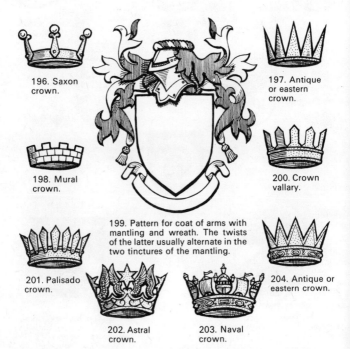

196. Saxon crown.

197. Antique or eastern crown.

198. Mural crown.

200. Crown vallary.

199. Pattern for coat of arms with mantling and wreath. The twists of the latter usually alternate in the two tinctures of the mantling.

201. Palisado crown.

202. Astral crown.

203. Naval crown.

204. Antique or eastern crown.

CRESTS

207. Crest of the German troubadour Frauenlob, about 1300.

205. Arms of the Count of Genevois, fourteenth century.

206. Arms of the Count of Savoy, fourteenth century.

The earliest use of a crest known to us comes from a seal dated 1197 belonging to Baldwin of Flanders. It was not until the thirteenth and fourteenth centuries that crests became general. They could be made of leather, canvas (on a wooden framework), feathers and suchlike, and were worn especially at tournaments. In Northern and Central Europe, and in the British Isles, most family coats of arms have a crest, but this is not the case in France and Southern Europe.

In many countries helmet and crest are not borne by women and the clergy.

208. Crest of the German emperor, about 1300.

209. Arms of the King of Sweden, about 1390.

CRESTS

210. The use of a crest may originally have denoted a certain rank, i.e. only people whose social position allowed participation in tournaments having the right to bear them.

In many cases crests bear no relation to the charges on the shield but in other cases they are similar or indentical. See Figs 211, 212 and 213.

211. Arms of the ancient baronial family of Rüdt von Collenberg.

212. Arms of the family of German industrialists von Borsig, ennobled in Prussia in 1909.

213. Arms of the old aristocratic German family of von Hassendorff.

CRESTS

214. Buffalo horns without a wreath.

215. An eagle on a wreath.

216. A demi-lion (double-queued) upon a wreath.

217. In England and Scotland a hat as shown here — called a cap of maintenance — is usually associated with a feudal title or privilege.

218. The armorial bearings of the German poet Friedrich von Schiller (1759–1805) as a member of the nobility of the Holy Roman Empire or *Reichsadel* (from 1802). The laurel wreath on the helmet symbolises his title of poet laureate.

219. As a rule wreath and coronet are alternatives but in Italy both are often used together, as on this helmet for a patrician. See also pp. 127 ff.

CRESTS

220. Coronet and three ostrich feathers.

221. Coronet and wings conjoined.

222. Coronet and vambraced arm with sword.

223. In several countries on the Continent a purely decorative coronet which does not pertain to any particular rank is used as a crest coronet. If it is placed on the shield, however, it is a sign of nobility. See Figs 394 and 512.

224. A purely decorative coronet set either on the helmet or used as a charge on the shield (see Fig. 338) is sometimes called a ducal coronet, though it does not necessarily indicate ducal or any other rank.

225. The crest of the British royal arms (as borne in England by H. M. Queen Elizabeth) consists of a crowned lion statant guardant on the royal crown. See also Fig. 309.

CRESTS

226. To show a helmet affronty and the crest in profile is considered bad heraldry. The helmet and crest should both face the same way where practicable.

227. A bishop's mitre as crest does not necessarily mean that the bearer is a bishop.

228. At times the crest and mantling become one. See also Figs 207, 213 and 226.

229. Arms of the German composer Karl Maria von Weber (1786–1826).

230. Arms of the Swedish explorer Sven Hedin (1865–1952), ennobled in 1902.

M = man.
W = wife.
Mo = man's mother

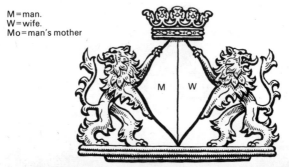

231. The arms of a married couple may be marshalled in various ways.
Above is the pattern for a Swedish countess.

233. Pattern for the arms
of a noble lady. She may
also bear her husband's
arms alone.

232. Pattern for the mar-
shalled arms of a married
couple, ensigned by the
husband's coronet, in this
instance a Swedish baron-
ial coronet.

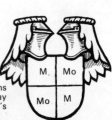

234. In England a man ma
quarter his paternal arm
with his mother's if she
an heraldic heiress, thoug
a second crest is normal
assumed only by Roy
Licence.

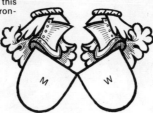

235. A pattern for the marshalled arms of a married couple. When for aesthetic
reasons and *de courtoise* the man's helmet and crest are turned towards the wife's,
the charges on the shield itself may follow suit.

ARMS OF ALLIANCE ETC.

M = man.
W = wife.

236. Pattern for an unmarried lady of the Swedish nobility. See also next page.

237. Pattern for an Anglican bishop: diocesan arms on the dexter, family arms on the sinister.

238. Pattern for a widow, Great Britain.

239. Pattern for a married lady of the Swedish nobility.

240. Pattern for an English gentleman married to a peeress in her own right.

241: Pattern for an untitled maiden lady.

242. Pattern for a Knight of Justice of the German Order of St John. The family arms are borne in the second and third quarters.

243. Pattern for a British widow without near male relations to carry on the line.

244. Pattern for a magnate of the Order of Malta. The family arms appear in the lower part of the shield.

ARMS OF WOMEN

245. Fictitious armorial bearings for a British peeress in her own right. No helmet or crest.

246. From the beginning of the sixteenth century it became the fashion in Great Britain and Western Europe to depict the arms of women on a lozenge-shaped escutcheon, but it never became general practice, and in Germany and Scandinavia the lozenge is hardly ever used.

247. An oval shield, or cartouche, is sometimes used, especially by church dignitaries (see Figs 873, 885, 889) and, in Napoleonic heraldry, by women (see Figs 483 and 484).

248. Fictitious armorial bearings for a woman who is head of a Scots clan. Crest and wreath without helmet, and a motto.

BADGES AND EMBLEMS

See the text on the next page.

249. Emblem of the French Queen Catherine de Medici (1519–89) when widowed. Her husband, King Henry II, was killed in a tournament in 1559. The Latin motto means 'Hence my tears, hence my sorrow'.

250. A sprig of broom, *planta genista*, was the badge of Geoffrey of Anjou (1113–51) and his descendants on the English throne, and it was from this that they took the name Plantagenet.

251. Emblem of Charles IX, King of France 1560–74. The two entwined columns relate to the Latin motto 'With piety and justice'.

252. Badge of Catherine of Aragon (1485–1536), Henry VIII's first queen: a Tudor rose, i.e. usually a white rose charged on a red one, here placed on a pomegranate (see Fig. 639).

253. The English Tudor dynasty had several badges, among them a portcullis, often shown crowned.

254. Badge of Bloody Mary: a Tudor rose for England and a sheaf of arrows for Spain (see Fig. 271).

255. Badge of Arthur, Prince of Wales (1486–1502).

BADGES AND EMBLEMS

A badge is a figure or a device which in some cases can be used in the same way as a coat of arms, but it is not emblazoned on a shield and need not always be in any special colours. The earliest badges are probably older than systematic heraldry, and some may have been perpetuated as charges in early escutcheons. Both escutcheon and badge may be used at the same time, in some cases together as in Fig. 271, where Spain's royal arms are accompanied by two royal badges, a sheaf of arrows and a yoke.

Badges were common in Southern Europe and France; in Great Britain they always were, and are still, much in favour, their use having been revived early this century, but this is not the case in Germany and Scandinavia, where there is no native word for the term 'badge'. In England badges were also borne by retainers or partisans of certain personages, and became in fact almost party emblems. In the Middle Ages the two rival lines of the royal house took their names from their badges, as did the royal dynasty itself (see Fig. 250). The white rose of York and the red rose of Lancaster were united in 1485 to form the red and white Tudor rose (see Fig. 261). Other British badges based on plants can be seen on p. 70. In modern times badges are used extensively by institutions such as schools, regiments, clubs and so on.

A badge therefore is often used by a large number of persons who are not of the same family but have another form of mutual relationship. But from the fifteenth century onwards another type developed which, while resembling the badge, was in many respects quite different. This was a personal device or cognizance often consisting of a motto and a figure alluding to it which together would represent a person and express something about his character, ideals, interests and so on. See Figs. 249, 251, 255 and 256. Most of these devices referred originally to an individual, not to a family, but many of them were subsequently used by the descendants of the first owner. Heraldic language also changed and the word 'device' came in some countries to mean only a motto without any emblem.

An Italian form of the device is the *impresa*, the content of which was often full of learned and fanciful references. In the sixteenth and seventeenth centuries the device and the *impresa* developed into what are called emblems. An emblem is a heraldic device or a symbolic or allegorical representation, often combined with a motto or slogan and as a rule of a religious or philosophical nature. Sometimes an emblem was quite a rebus, with Latin, Greek or Hebrew words and letters mixed with charges full of symbolism and subtlety.

The dividing line between badge, device, *impresa* and emblem is difficult to draw, and on these pages we have endeavoured to avoid using the ambiguous word 'device' and have kept mainly to the terms 'badge' and 'emblem'. See the Luther rose, Fig. 903.†

† In modern English heraldry the terms 'badge', 'motto' and 'rebus' have precise technical meanings, whereas the terms 'emblem' and 'device' are used more loosely—Ed.

BADGES AND EMBLEMS

256. Emblem of the Roman noble family of Piccolomini. The crescent comes from their coat of arms and the Latin motto means 'Immaculate'.

257. A chained white hart lodged ducally collared and chained gold was the badge of Richard II, King of England 1377–99.

258. Badge of the English nobleman Roger de Lasci (Constable of Chester, 1179–1211).

259. The 'Savoy Knot', emblem of the ruling house of Savoy. See also the collar of the Order of Chivalry in Fig. 670.

260. Emblem of the dukes of Burgundy and of the Order of the Golden Fleece established by them: branches, forged steel and sparks.

261. Badge of the English royal house: a rose crowned. The flower is a combination of the white rose badge of York and the red rose of Lancaster and is called a Tudor rose.

262. A hedgehog crowned was the emblem of the house of Orleans, a line of the French royal house, whose best known member was Francis I, King of France 1515–47.

BANNERS

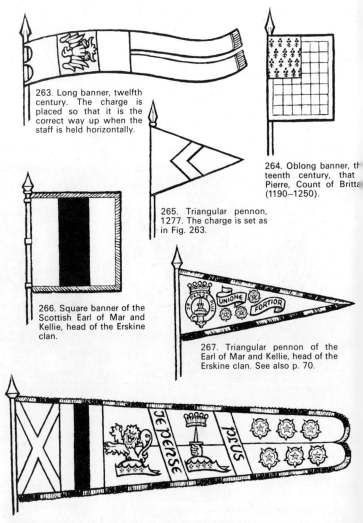

263. Long banner, twelfth century. The charge is placed so that it is the correct way up when the staff is held horizontally.

264. Oblong banner, thirteenth century, that of Pierre, Count of Brittany (1190–1250).

265. Triangular pennon, 1277. The charge is set as in Fig. 263.

266. Square banner of the Scottish Earl of Mar and Kellie, head of the Erskine clan.

267. Triangular pennon of the Earl of Mar and Kellie, head of the Erskine clan. See also p. 70.

268. Standard of the Earl of Mar and Kellie, head of the Erskine clan. See also Figs 217 and 362.

SUPPORTERS

In some instances a coat of arms may be held up or carried by supporters. In most cases there are two (identical or different), but from time to time only one, and in exceptional cases more than two, are used. Most supporters are animals or fabulous creatures, but human beings or creatures in human form are also used quite frequently. Supporters began to appear regularly in the fifteenth century. They may have developed from the figures which seal engravers placed between the shield in the middle of the seal and the text around the edge. Another origin may be found in the cavalcade or presentations that took place before a tournament, when the armorial shields of the participants were carried round by their pages.

269. An angel supporter.

270. Arms of the Hanseatic town of Bremen.

SUPPORTERS

271. Armorial bearings of Isabella of Castile (castle and lion) and Ferdinand of Aragon (pallets and eagles). At the base is the pomegranate of Granada. The shield is supported by a crowned eagle. The yoke and the sheaf of arrows beneath are Spanish royal emblems.

In some countries everybody is entitled to use supporters and these need not always be the same ones.

The question of whether one's shield should be supported by a mermaid, two elephants or something else is decided on purely decorative grounds.

In other countries there are rules as to who is entitled to them – the high nobility, towns of a certain size, members of certain orders – and once supporters have been decided on, others cannot be used: their use is not obligatory though, for an escutcheon can always be depicted without supporters.

Some supporters stand on a natural base or 'compartment', others on a plinth, an ornament or a motto-scroll.

272. Arms of the Earl of Snowdon. The shield is supported by a griffin and an eagle.

SUPPORTERS

273. Arms of the Anglo-Belgian painter and lithographer James Ensor (1860–1949) who was created a Baron by the King of the Belgians in 1930. The supporters are two mermaids, each with the clef of G in her hand. The mermaids, like the sea in the top half of the shield, may be symbolic of Ostend, Ensor's birth place, and the beach where he played in his childhood.

274. Arms of the Russian aristocratic family of Mendeleyev, of which Dimitri Mendeleyev (1834–1907), the well-known chemist, was a member. The supporters are two lions rampant reguardant.

THE PAVILION AND THE
ROBE OF ESTATE

275. Pavilion, favoured by some hereditary sovereigns and reserved exclusively for their use.

276. Robe of estate of continental type.

277. Robe of estate for Napoleonic counts and senators.

The origins of the robe of estate can be traced back at least to the sixteenth century. Used sometimes as an alternative to mantling, it stems perhaps from the robes of honour or office that princes and important officials wore on ceremonial occasions or from the draperies around a throne. The robe of estate is especially used by princes, the high aristocracy and the holders of certain important offices, but not by all in these categories.

THE ROBE OF ESTATE

278. Arms of the Sovereign Military Order of Malta.

The outside of a robe of estate is usually purple or red, but may also be black or blue, as found at times in Sweden and France. It sometimes has a pattern of fleurs-de-lys, crowns or Napoleonic bees (see pp. 82 and 90) or repeats the charges from the arms (Fig. 464). The inside is usually ermine, but yellow (gold) and white (silver) may also be used.

279. Arms of the Prioress du Plessis de Richelieu, with insignia of office including staff and robe; eighteenth century.

280. Robe of estate of a Spanish grandee with pattern for the escutcheon.

AUGMENTATIONS

An augmentation is an addition, i.e. a supplementary charge which a ruler adds to an already existing coat of arms to honour its bearer. The augmentation often consists of the sovereign's own bearings or a part thereof, or some other national symbol.

281. A chief with the principal charge of Belgium's arms (see p. 80), used as an augmentation by Belgian kings.

282. Augmentation for the Duke of Wellington after his victory over Napoleon: the Union Badge placed as an inescutcheon on Wellington's paternal arms. (The lions in the second and third quarters are usually shown with coronets about their necks.)

283. Another form of augmentation used by the kings of Belgium: a chief made up of the Belgian flag.

284. In 1465 King Louis II of France gave the Italian Piero de' Medici permission to replace the topmost red roundel in the Medici arms with the arms of France, three gold fleurs-de-lys, set on a blue roundel.

285. The red fess with the badge of the Order signifies that the bearer is a Knight of the Legion of Honour. Napoleon's augmentation for Cuvier, 1811.

286. Arms of the French city of Clermont-Ferrand. The four fleurs-de-lys are a royal augmentation to the city's original arms.

INSIGNIA OF OFFICE

287. Bishop's crosier. Shown here as used by Benedict de Montferrand, Bishop of Lausanne 1476–91.

288. Arms of the province of Brandenburg in Prussia. The blue inescutcheon with sceptre became from 1466 the insignia of the Lord High Chamberlains of the Holy Roman Empire, the *Erzkämmerer*, namely the Margraves of Brandenburg.

289. A staff as insignia of Ireland's Lord High Steward, here a member of the Talbot family.

290. Two crossed banners behind the family arms of Scotland's Royal Standard Bearer. (The arms are those of Scrymgeour.)

291. Two batons in saltire for England's Earl Marshal, the Duke of Norfolk.

292. Two crossed crosiers behind the official coat of arms of the Hereditary Keeper of St Fillan's Crosier in Scotland.

293. Arms of the German Counts zu Pappenheim. The two crossed swords on a black and white field are their insignia as Hereditary Marshals to the Holy Roman Empire.

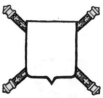

294. Two crossed Field Marshal's batons for the Marshals of the Kingdom of France.

295. An anchor for the Admirals of the Kingdom of France.

Insignia such as these are the distinguishing marks of power or dignity pertaining to an office. They may be emblazoned with the pertinent arms, be set behind or about the shield, or be part of a special official coat of arms.

296. Two sets of sword and belt for the Master of the Horse, the *Grand Écuyer*, of the Kingdom of France.

297. Two crossed batons for the Marshal of Sweden.

INSIGNIA OF OFFICE

298. Mantle, crown and crossed batons for the Commander in Chief, *Capitán General*, of the Kingdom of Spain.

299. Crown and anchor for the Commander of the Galleys, *General de Galera*, of the Kingdom of Spain.

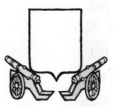

300. The sceptre of Charles X in 1804, with the hand of justice.

301. Two cannon for the *General de Artileria* of the Kingdom of Spain.

302. Sceptre made for the Sacristy of Chartres in 1594, with fleur-de-lys.

BLAZONING

303. Arms of the English poet Geoffrey Chaucer (c. 1340–1400): per pale argent and gules, a bend counterchanged.

304. Arms of the English family of More of which Sir Thomas More (1478–1535) was a member: argent a chevron engrailed between three moor-cocks sable, crested gules. (The moorcocks are a pun on the surname.)

305. Arms of the English politician Benjamin Disraeli (1804–81): per saltire gules and argent, a tower triple towered in chief proper, two lions rampant in fess sable and an eagle displayed in base or.

By the blazon we mean a detailed technical description of a coat of arms sufficient to enable an artist conversant with the language of heraldry to depict it accurately. The order in which different parts of the achievement should be described may be found in standard manuals of heraldry.

306. Arms of the Spectacle Makers' Company, London. Vert a chevron or between three pairs of nose-spectacles proper, framed of the second. Crest: on a wreath or and vert, two arms embowed vested vert cuffed or, the hands proper holding a sun in splendour within an annulet gold. Supporters: on either side a falcon proper belled or and charged with a sword erect gules.

BLAZONING

Shield: Or a chevron gules, on a chief sable a label of the first.
Crest: On a wreath or and gules, a griffin rampant of the first.
Banners: Flanking the crest two banners, the staffs light brown with silver finials and ferrules passing behind the shield and extending below the motto scroll, the dexter banner or bordered compony of the like and azure, charged with a mullet of the last voided argent: the sinister banner or bordered compony of the like and gules, charged with a Tudor rose barbed and seeded vert.
Scroll: Or lined sable with lettering of the last. Motto: *Aegis Fortissima Honos* ('Honour is the strongest shield'). (This is the official blazon supplied by the Department of the Army—Ed.)

307. Arms of the Institute of Heraldry, part of the United States Army.

308. Arms of Eton College, the English public school.

Sable three lilies slipped and leaved argent; on a chief per pale azure and gules a fleur-de-lys and a lion passant guardant or.
Motto: *Floreat Etona* (May Eton flourish).

GREAT BRITAIN

309. The British royal arms (version for Parliamentary use). The shield is made up of the arms of England (first and fourth quarters), gules three lions passant guardant or; Scotland (second quarter), or a lion rampant within a double tressure flory counter-flory gules, see Fig. 363; and Ireland (third quarter), azure a harp or stringed argent.
Surrounding the shield is the Order of the Garter with the French motto *Honi soit qui mal y pense* ('Evil to him who evil thinketh'). It is ensigned by the royal crown and in this version the crest is omitted.
Supporters: for England a crowned lion; for Scotland a unicorn with a crown about its neck and chained. Motto in French *Dieu et mon droit* ('God and my right').

310. The arms of the city of Canterbury.

311. The arms of the city of Salisbury (usually depicted as azure four bars or).

312. The arms of Stratford-upon-Avon.

GREAT BRITAIN

313. Arms of an English duke: John Churchill,
Duke of Marlborough (1650–1722), Knight of
the Garter.

314. Arms of the
mathematician and
philosopher Sir
Isaac Newton
(1642–1727).

315. Arms of
Durham County
Council.

316. Arms of the
Quaker William
Penn (1644–1718),
the founder of
Pennsylvania.

GREAT BRITAIN

317. Pattern for the arms of a gentleman (esquire), Scottish model.

318. Pattern for the arms of a British baronet; without the inescutcheon argent charged with a sinister hand couped at the wrist and erect gules it is that of a knight.

319. Pattern for the arms of a gentleman (esquire), English model.

320. Arms of the city of Liverpool.

321. Arms of the city of Oxford (the ox normally has gold horns and hooves).

322. Pattern of the arms of a British peer, usually meaning a member of the House of Lords. The coronet (see p. 68) rests on the shield, and the helmet or helmets (with crest) on the coronet.

GREAT BRITAIN

323. Arms of the City of London.

324. Arms of the writer Jonathan Swift (1667–1745).

325. Arms of the former London County Council.

326. Arms of the writer Henry Fielding (1707–45).

327. Arms of an English knight, Sir Winston Churchill, Knight of the Garter.
In England the number of helmets has nothing to do with rank but is dependent on arms combined on the shield.

328. Arms of an English baron, the poet Lord Byron (1788–1824). See also Fig. 322. The English aristocracy, whose members are called peers and are usually members of the House of Lords, consists of five classes: dukes, marquesses, earls, viscounts and barons; the last four are also called lords, and a baron is only known by that title in common parlance.

GREAT BRITAIN

329. A typical coat of arms
for a British knight. These
are those of Sir Charles
Redvers Westlake.

330. Arms of the states-
man Sir Robert Peel
(1788–1850). The hand
indicates that he was a
baronet.

331. Badge of Ulster,
borne in the arms of
baronets (except those of
Novia Scotia, see Fig.
364).

332. Arms of the poet Sir
Walter Scott (1771-1832).
Note the baronet's shield
in the centre.

GREAT BRITAIN

333. Arms* of an English gentleman, the father of Jane Austen, the authoress (1775–1817).

334. Arms of the city of Plymouth.

335. Arms of the city of Portsmouth.

336. Arms of the Worshipful Company of Vintners. (The car' wheel on the sail shoul be gold.)

*The coat tentatively attributed to Jane Austen's family in *Historic Heraldry* by A. R. Wagner is a different one, namely 'Argent on a chevron between three lions' gambs erased sable three bezants'—Ed.

GREAT BRITAIN

337. Arms of Charles Edgar Hires, Bryn Mawr, Pennsylvania, U.S.A. (The swords in the crest should be gold throughout.)

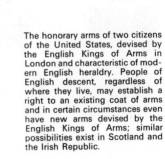

338. Arms of Lorenzo Simmons Winslow, Washington D.C., U.S.A.

The honorary arms of two citizens of the United States, devised by the English Kings of Arms in London and characteristic of modern English heraldry. People of English descent, regardless of where they live, may establish a right to an existing coat of arms and in certain circumstances even have new arms devised by the English Kings of Arms; similar possibilities exist in Scotland and the Irish Republic.

GREAT BRITAIN

339. Coronet of the heir-apparent to the throne, the Prince of Wales. (The two outermost gems in this and in the royal crown are normally coloured blue.)

340. Queen Elizabeth's crown (the royal crown). See also Fig. 309.

341. Coronet for the Sovereign's sons and daughters (except the heir-apparent) and brothers and sisters.

342. Coronet for dukes and duchesses (see also Figs 313 and 366).

343. Coronet for Kings of Arms, the principal heraldic officers of the College of Arms.

344. Coronet for marquesses and their wives.

345. Coronet for earls and their wives (see also Figs 272 and 367).

346. Coronet for viscounts and their wives (see also Fig. 322).

347. Coronet for barons and baronesses (see also Figs 245, 328, 358 and 369).

The crowns and coronets actually worn by the royal family and by some ranks of the nobility are in some cases rather different from those illustrated on this page. When used as a mark of rank the coronets are often depicted without the red cap. Baronets and knights do not have coronets.

SCOTLAND

348. Arms of the City of Edinburgh.

In Britain some cities and towns have crest, supporters and motto, as shown here. The thistles on the compartment are Scotland's national flower, see Fig. 352.

349. Arms of Bruce, Earl of Elgin.

350. Arms of Douglas, Earl of Douglas.

351. Arms of Stuart, Marquess of Bute.

SCOTLAND

Badges representing plants (see also p. 46)

352. Thistle.

353. Oak.

354. Holly.

355. Juniper.

356. Mistletoe.

357. Ivy.

358.

359.

360.

361.

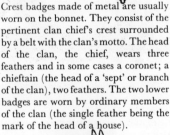

Crest badges made of metal are usually worn on the bonnet. They consist of the pertinent clan chief's crest surrounded by a belt with the clan's motto. The head of the clan, the chief, wears three feathers and in some cases a coronet; a chieftain (the head of a 'sept' or branch of the clan), two feathers. The two lower badges are worn by ordinary members of the clan (the single feather being the mark of the head of a house).

362. The royal badge: the cross of St Andrew and coronet.

363. The Scottish royal arms.

364. Badge of a baronet of Nova Scotia.

365. Chieftain with badge on his bonnet.

SCOTLAND

366. Arms of the Duke of Argyll, chief of the Campbell clan. The baton and sword behind the shield are his insignia as Hereditary Great Master of the Household and High Justiciar of Scotland. The baton is normally red and the hilt of the sword is usually in base.

367. Arms of Hay, Earl of Erroll, chief of the Hay clan.

368. Arms of the borough of Rothesay, granted 1925. (The mural crown should be stone-coloured.)

369. Arms of Forbes, Lord Forbes, chief of the Forbes clan.

71

ENGLAND AND SCOTLAND

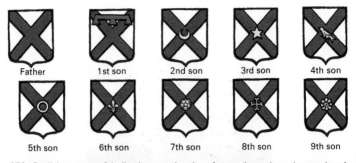

Father	1st son	2nd son	3rd son	4th son
5th son	6th son	7th son	8th son	9th son

370. English system of indicating sons' order of precedence by using marks of cadency. One example of this is shown in Fig. 326, but the system has never been used very extensively.

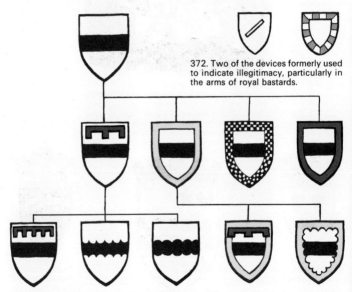

372. Two of the devices formerly used to indicate illegitimacy, particularly in the arms of royal bastards.

371. In Scotland another system of 'differencing' the arms of sons in one or more generations has been worked out. This chart gives an approximate idea of the system, though it should be mentioned that the labels are generally used only temporarily while the other differences are permanent.

IRELAND

374. Arms of the city of Dublin (*baile Atha Cliath*).

373. Ireland's coat of arms. It is also the third quartering in the British royal arms—see Fig. 309.

375. Arms of the four provinces of Leinster, Connaught, Ulster and Munster.

376. Arms of John Fitzgerald Kennedy (1917—63), President of the United States, granted him by the Chief Herald of Ireland in 1961.

IRELAND

377. O'Donnell.

378. Fitzpatrick.

379. Fitzgerald.

380. Lynch.

Examples of arms belonging to
famous Irish families of Gaelic or
Norman origin.

381. O'Monahan.

382. MacNamara.

383. O'Shea.

384. Walsh (Iverk).

IRELAND

Two typical modern Irish coats of arms granted by the Chief Herald of Ireland to American citizens of Irish descent.

385. Arms of Bishop McCauley, Silversprings, Maryland.

386. Arms of Joseph Robert Carroll, Toledo, Ohio.

THE NETHERLANDS

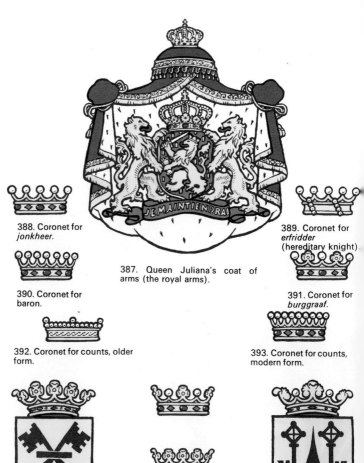

388. Coronet for *jonkheer.*

389. Coronet for *erfridder* (hereditary knight)

390. Coronet for baron.

387. Queen Juliana's coat of arms (the royal arms).

391. Coronet for *burggraaf.*

392. Coronet for counts, older form.

393. Coronet for counts, modern form.

394 (*above*) and 395. Counts' and marquis' coronets, as used in civic heraldry—see Figs 396 and 397.

396. City arms of Waddingsveen, with coronet of a marquis.

397. City arms of Anloo, with coronet of a count.

THE NETHERLANDS

398. City arms of Amsterdam.

Below are shown some other city arms:

399. Zeven-
bergen.

400. Nieuwer-
Amstel.

401. Almelo.

402. Maastricht.

403. Alkmaar.

404. Groningen.

405. Dordrecht.

THE NETHERLANDS

406. Arms of the province of Gelderland.

407. City arms
of Bergen

409. Arms of the province of Utrecht.

408. City arms
of Grave.

410. Coronet of
a prince.

411. Coronet of
a duke.

THE NETHERLANDS

412. Coat of arms of Prince Claus of the Netherlands: first and fourth quarters the Netherlands lion (see Fig. 387), second and third quarters the arms of the family of von Amsberg.

413. Arms of the non-aristocratic family of Warnsinck.

414. Arms of the aristocratic family of Trip.

BELGIUM

415. Coat of arms of Queen Elisabeth, a Bavarian princess married to King Albert of Belgium. The Belgian royal arms, on a field sable a lion or, can be seen dexter, her ancestral Bavarian arms sinister.

416. Coronet of a Baron of Brabant (*baron brabancon*).

417. City arms of Brussels.

418. Coronet of a viscount.

BELGIUM

419. City arms
of Bruges.

420. Pattern for the arms of a nobleman
without title (*écuyer* or *jonkheer*).

421. City arms
of Antwerp.

422. Pattern for arms of hereditary
knight (*chevalier* or *erfridder*).

423. Pattern for
arms of a count.

FRANCE

424. The French royal arms as used during the reign of Louis XVIII (1814/15–1824). Behind the shield, which is encircled by the collars of the Orders of St Michael and the Holy Spirit, are two crossed sceptres.

425. Coronet for royal princes and princesses.

426. Crown of the heir to the throne, the *Dauphin*.

427. Coronet for the king's illegitimate children.

428. Coronet for dukes and duchesses. See Fig. 464.

FRANCE

429. Arms of the city of Paris. The Latin motto means 'She pitches and rolls but does not sink'. Beneath the shield are the badges of the Legion of Honour (centre), the Order of Liberation (dexter) and the War Cross (1939–45).

430. Arms of the astrologer Michel de Nostre-Dame, also called Nostradamus (1503–66).

431. Arms of the writer Michel Eyquem, Seigneur de Montaigne (1533–92), according to his *Essais*.

432. During the French Revolution, from 1789, all traditional heraldry was abolished, and the French Republic has no definite coat of arms. The device shown here is one of several used nowadays. It would normally be shown within the collar of the Legion of Honour.

FRANCE

433. Coronet for marquises, older form.

434. Coronet of a duke and *pair de France.*

435. Coronet for counts, older form.

436. Coronet for marquises, more recent form—see Fig. 466.

437. Coronet for princes not of royal blood.

438. Coronet for counts, more recent form.

439. Coronet for viscounts, older form.

441. Coronet for barons, older form.

442. Coronet for viscounts, more recent form.

440. Helmet and crown as used by the king.

443. Coronet for barons, more recent form.

FRANCE

445. Crown of eleventh century, changed by order of Saint Louis (relics inserted).

444. Arms of the heir to the throne, *le Dauphin de Viennois*, in their fifteenth-century form. The four coats of arms on this page are all variations of the royal arms, see Fig. 424.

446. Arms of the Duke of Bourbon, thirteenth century.

447. Arms of the Duke of Anjou, fourteenth century.

448. Arms of the Duke of Orléans, fifteenth century.

FRANCE

Duvernoy

de Carpentier

Silvestre
de Sacy

de Crozé
de Clesmes

Courlet
de Vregille

Wignier
d'Avesnes

Méniolle
d'Haut-
huille

de Lucy
de Pélissac

Doë de
Maindre-
ville

Préveraud
de Vaumas

449. Above are examples of variations on a heraldic theme. There is in some cases a family relationship or a feudal connection behind such similar arms, but often the similarity occurs by chance. In France there may be another reason, for in the 1690s the authorities tried to compel all citizens to assume coats of arms (at the same time levying taxes on them), and as a result coats of arms were produced in such numbers that it was difficult to make them distinguishable from each other.

450. City arms
of Strasbourg.

453. Arms of
the Duchy of
Lorraine.

451. City arms
of Metz.

452. City arms
of Lunéville.

454. City arms
of Poitiers.

FRANCE

455. City arms of Rouen.

456. City arms of Orléans.

457. City arms of Limoges.

It is very common in France for arms of larger towns to have a blue chief with three golden fleurs-de-lys or, in the older form, semy of fleurs-de-lys. See Paris, Fig. 429, and also Fig. 286.

458. Arms of the composer Jean-Philippe Rameau (1683–1764), who was posthumously ennobled in 1765.

Since the Renaissance crests have played a less important role in France than in most other countries. Many families bore nothing on their helmets, and titled nobility often merely had coronets, set either on the helmet or on the shield itself (see the following page). By the eighteenth century the helmet as well as the crest had largely disappeared from French heraldry.

459. Pattern for a duke and *pair de France* when France was a kingdom. The charge on the shield was frequently repeated on the mantle (see Figs 446, 447 and 464). Crest, supporters and motto may be added, and this is also the case with Figs 460 and 462.

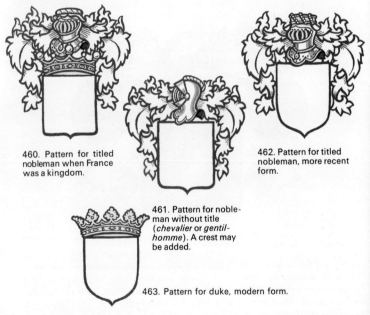

460. Pattern for titled nobleman when France was a kingdom.

462. Pattern for titled nobleman, more recent form.

461. Pattern for nobleman without title (*chevalier* or *gentilhomme*). A crest may be added.

463. Pattern for duke, modern form.

FRANCE

464. Arms of the statesman Cardinal Armand-Jean du Plessis de Richelieu (1585–1642). The red prelate's hat with tassels shows he was a cardinal, the coronet that he was a duke, the anchor that he was an admiral, the badge that he was a Knight of the Order of the Holy Spirit.

465. Arms of the prominent Huguenot Admiral Gaspard de Coligny (1519–72). Surrounding the shield is the collar of the Order of St Michael.

466. Arms of the champion of liberty and statesman, the Marquis de La Fayette (1757–1834). Below the shield is the Order of St Louis.

467. Arms of Napoleon I and Napoleon III as Emperors of the French. Compare the royal arms, Fig. 424. The fleurs-de-lys have been replaced by an eagle standing on a thunderbolt (the colours are the same) from a Roman prototype, see Fig. 11, and on the mantling bees have taken the place of the fleurs-de-lys, see also Figs 472 and 487. The Legion of Honour has supplanted the royal orders, but apart from that the arms look much the same.

When the French Revolution started in 1789, all traditional heraldry, as mentioned before, was abolished and prohibited. After Napoleon had made himself Emperor in 1804 and created an imperial aristocracy, he himself introduced a new imperial heraldry. The coronet was replaced by a system of caps to denote rank and even the charges on the shield were subject to a certain system, as were the other appurtenances of the armorial bearings.

NAPOLEONIC HERALDRY

468. Napoleon I's heraldic crown as King of Italy, 1805-14.

469. The original arms of the Buonaparte family.

470. The heraldic royal crown of the Napoleonic period as used in Westphalia and Spain, 1807/8-1813.

471. Pattern for a Napoleonic sovereign prince.

472. Pattern for a non-sovereign prince (*prince grand dignitaire*).

473. Heraldic cap for non-sovereign prince.

474. Heraldic cap for duke.

475. Heraldic cap for count.

476. Heraldic cap for baron.

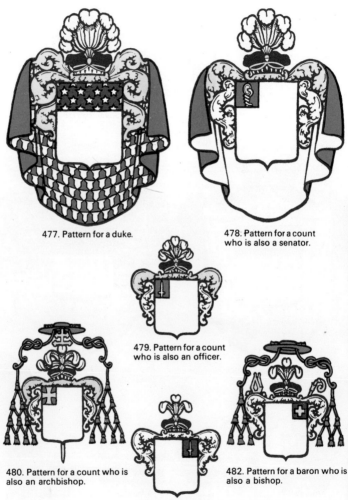

477. Pattern for a duke.

478. Pattern for a count who is also a senator.

479. Pattern for a count who is also an officer.

480. Pattern for a count who is also an archbishop.

481. Pattern for a baron who is also an officer.

482. Pattern for a baron who is also a bishop.

NAPOLEONIC HERALDRY

483. Pattern for a woman created countess in her own right.

484. Pattern for a woman created baroness in her own right.

485. Pattern for a *Chevalier d'Empire* who is also a Knight of the Legion of Honour.

487. Pattern for a city of first grade of importance. Cf. Figs 455–7.

486. Pattern for a *Chevalier d'Empire*.

488. Pattern for a city of second grade of importance.

489. Pattern for a city of third grade of importance.

GERMANY

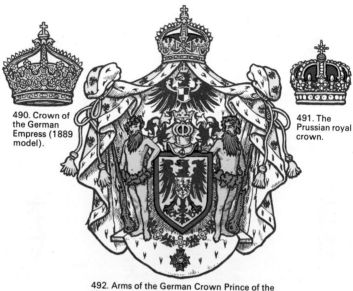

490. Crown of the German Empress (1889 model).

491. The Prussian royal crown.

492. Arms of the German Crown Prince of the House of Hohenzollern. The shield is surrounded by the collar of the Order of the Black Eagle.

493. Arms of East Germany, The *Deutsche Demokratische Republik,* from 1955.

494. Arms of West Germany, The *Bundesrepublik Deutschland,* from 1950.

495. The German imperial crown, 1889.

GERMANY

496. Arms of the statesman Otto von Bismarck (1815–98) as Prussian prince.

497. Arms of the
Landkreis Ansbach
(from 1955).

498. Arms of the
Landkreis Böblingen
(from 1948).

499. Arms of the
Landkreis Villingen
(from 1958).

GERMANY

500. Royal crown.

501. Crown of Grand Duke or royal crown prince.

502. Crown of duke or younger royal prince.

503. Ducal crown of different form. See also Fig. 502.

504. Crown of Elector.

505. Cap of Elector.

506. Dukes in Bavaria and of Württemberg etc.

507. Crowns of heirs to the throne of ducal ruling houses.

508. Crown for a prince.

509. Another form of crown for princes. See also Fig. 508. The royal and princely crowns usually rested directly on the shield (as shown here) or were above the robe of estate, as in Figs 492 and 496.

510. Coronet for counts who were formerly sovereign rulers.

GERMANY

511. Coronet of baron, older form.

512 and 513. Coronets for untitled nobility for use without helmet. (That in Fig. 512 can also be used on a helmet as a crest-coronet without indicating nobility.)

514. Coronet for count, older form.

515. Coronet for baron, more recent form. See Fig. 531.

516. Mural crown as used in civic heraldry.

517. Coronet for count, more recent form. See Fig. 521.

518. 'Small coat of arms' for the federal state of Bavaria, 1950.

520. Royal crown of the Middle Ages.

519. Arms for the federal state of Rhenish Palatinate, 1948. When Republican Germany uses a crown on a state coat of arms, it is called a 'people's crown' (*Volkskrone*).

97

GERMANY

521. Arms of the family of Zeppelin, of which the pioneer of airships, Count
Ferdinand von Zeppelin (1838–1917), was a member.

522. Neukölln.   523. Tempelhof.   524. Wilmersdorf.

Arms of three West Berlin boroughs. The charge on the mural crown is the civic
coat of Berlin.

GERMANY

525. Arms of the
Counts von
Buxhoeveden.

526. Arms of the
Counts von
Rechteren Limpurg.

527. Arms of the
Princes zu Waldburg.

Coronets, supporters, mottoes and robes of estate were not used in mediaeval heraldry, and families of ancient lineage such as the three above often forego such accessories, although they may have the right to use them.

528. City arms of
Heidelberg (1436).

529. City arms of
Bonn (from 1732).

530. Arms of the countly family of
von Spee, of which Admiral Maximilian
von Spee (1961–1914) was a member.

It was during the late Gothic period that the custom began of marshalling several escutcheons on one shield and using more than one helmet.

GERMANY

531. Arms of the baronial family of von Richthofen, of which the famous flying ace of the First World War, Manfred von Richthofen (1892–1918), was a member. Some titled noble families in Germany have supporters, others do not, and there exist no definite regulations regarding this.

532. City arms of Kaiserslautern, from the sixteenth century.

533. City arms of Coblenz, from the fourteenth century.

534. City arms of Trier, from the fifteenth century.

GERMANY

535. Arms of the ancient noble family of von Kleist, of which the poet Heinrich von Kleist (1777–1811) was a member.

536. City arms of Ulm, from the fourteenth century.

537. Arms of the author Johann Wolfgang von Goethe (1749–1832), raised to the *Reichsadel* of the Holy Roman Empire in 1782.

538. City arms of Aachen.

539. Arms of the poet Ernst von Wildenbruch (1845–1909).

540. City arms of Würzburg.

541. City arms of Stuttgart, from the fifteenth century.

GERMANY

542. Arms of the Barons von Lützow, one of whom was Ludwig, Baron von Lützow (1782–1834), who raised the *Freikorps Lützow* to fight against Napoleon.

543. Arms of the Barons von Eichendorff, among whom was the poet Josef, Baron von Eichendorff (1788–1857).

544. Arms of the painter and sculptor, Franz von Stuck (1863–1928), raised to the Bavarian nobility in 1906.

545. Arms of the noble family of von Steuben, used by the American general Friedrich von Steuben (1730–94), who took part in the American War of Independence.

GERMANY

546. Pattern for non-aristocratic arms with helmet affronty.

547. Pattern for non-aristocratic arms, with shield accouchy and helmet in profile.

During the Renaissance the chanceries of the various countries mostly used the barred helmet (see p. 18) for the arms of the nobility, in contrast to the tournament helmet for the non-aristocratic (as above). But many of the latter for that very reason bore the barred helmet. And many noblemen developed a preference for the tournament helmet because of the fact that it was an earlier type.

548. Arms of the philosopher Arthur Schopenhauer (1788–1860). The cartouche surround is a decorative feature and not a permanent component of the arms.

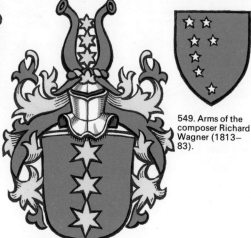

549. Arms of the composer Richard Wagner (1813–83).

550. Arms of the poet Eduard Mörike (1804–75).

GERMANY

Lind 1664   Ruidius 1517   Kra 1595   Fuchs 1679   Fries 1657   Bon 1604

551. It gradually became the custom to set the cipher on a shield. Only a few of these 'arms' were coloured.

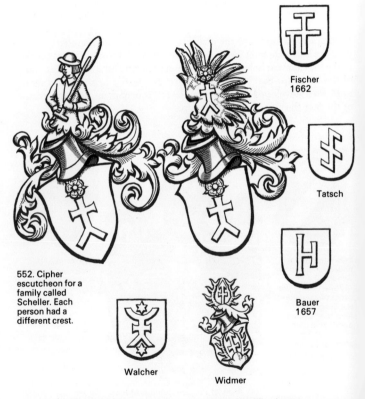

Fischer 1662

Tatsch

Bauer 1657

552. Cipher escutcheon for a family called Scheller. Each person had a different crest.

Walcher

Widmer

553. Combination of cipher and ordinary heraldic charges.

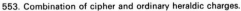

GERMANY

554. City arms of Munich.

557. Example of non-aristocratic arms, those of an uncle of the composer Johann Sebastian Bach (1685–1750).

555. City arms of Bautzen.

556. Arms of the family and province of Hohenzollern.

558. Arms of the Duchy of Saxony, later those of the Prussian province of the same name.

559. City arms of Königsberg in East Prussia (present-day Kaliningrad).

560. Arms of Berlin as a 'Land'.

561. City arms of Dresden.

GERMANY

562. Another example of a non-aristocratic coat of arms, that of the painter and engraver Albrecht Dürer (1471–1528).

563. City arms of Frankfurt am Main.

564. City arms of Wiesbaden.

565. City arms of Nuremberg as designed in about 1520. It is very rare, but not unheard of, for a city to have two coats of arms.

AUSTRIA

566. The 'genea-logical arms' of the house of Austria, with the original Habsburg lion device, Austria's white fess on a red field and the bend of the House of Lorraine. The archducal crown and the collar of the Order of the Golden Fleece ensign and surround the shield.

567. The 'small coat of arms' of Imperial Austria, 1915. The double-headed eagle of the Empire with the original arms of Austria as ines-cutcheon, ensigned by the Imperial crown.

568. Arms of the former duchy, now the province, of Lower Austria, ensigned by the archducal cap. The eagles should be arranged 2—2—1.

569. The archducal cap of Styria.

570. Arms of the Republic of Austria, 1945.

571. Arms of the province of Tyrol.

107

AUSTRIA

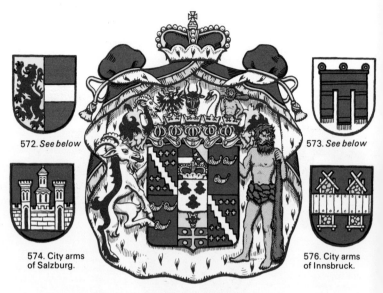

572. *See below*

573. *See below*

574. City arms
of Salzburg.

576. City arms
of Innsbruck.

575. Arms of an Austrian prince, the statesman
Klemens von Metternich (1773–1859).

572. (*above*)
Arms of the
province of
Salzburg.

573 (*above*)
Arms of the
province of
Vorarlberg.

577. Arms of the
Duchy of Carinthia,
fourteenth century.

578. Archducal cap.

579. Arms of the
Duchy of Styria,
fourteenth century.

AUSTRIA

580. Arms of Baron Rothschild, 1822. The inescutcheon is a pun on his name, 'Rothschild' meaning 'red shield'. (The red shield was originally the sign of the house where the family lived.) The Austrian eagle appears in the first quarter. The hand holding the arrows in the second and third quarters is no doubt meant to symbolise strength through solidarity and unity. Motto: 'Unity, Integrity, Industry'.

581. City arms of St Pölten, 1538. (The wolf should be shown brown.)

582. City arms of Wels.

583. City arms of Krems, 1463.

584. Arms of a hereditary knight, Ritter von Liszt, of Hungarian descent, the family of the composer Franz Liszt (1811–86).

From the time of the reign of Charles VI (1711–40) to the collapse of the Empire in 1918 hundreds of hereditary knights were created, nearly all of whom bore two helmets above the coat of arms.

585. City arms of Klagenfurt, fourteenth century.

586. City arms of Linz.

AUSTRIA

587. Vienna's coat of arms as granted to the city by Emperor Frederick III in 1461 (the inescutcheon being added in 1464). Today the inescutcheon is generally used alone.

588. Arms of the Kingdom of Galicia under the old Austro-Hungarian monarchy.

589. Arms of the Margravate of Istria under the old Austro-Hungarian monarchy.

590. Arms of the Austrian *Oberstfeldarzt* (Surgeon General) Matthäus von Mederer und Wuthwehr, raised to the nobility by Emperor Joseph II in 1789.

SWITZERLAND

591. Arms of the canton of Zürich.

592. Arms of the canton of Fribourg.

593. The Swiss coat of arms, dating from 1814 but resembling the colours of the Bern cavalry in the thirteenth century.

594. Arms of the canton of Zug.

595. Arms of the canton of Lucerne.

596. Arms of the canton of Bern.

597. Arms of the canton of Uri.

598. Arms of the physician Theophrastus Bombastus von Hohenheim, also called Paracelsus (1493–1541).

599. Arms of the canton of Glarus.

600. Arms of the canton of Geneva.

SWITZERLAND

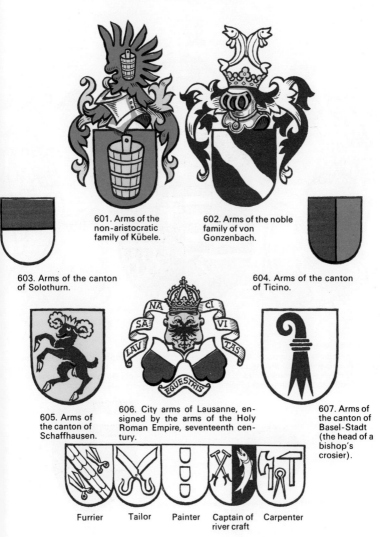

601. Arms of the non-aristocratic family of Kübele.

602. Arms of the noble family of von Gonzenbach.

603. Arms of the canton of Solothurn.

604. Arms of the canton of Ticino.

605. Arms of the canton of Schaffhausen.

606. City arms of Lausanne, ensigned by the arms of the Holy Roman Empire, seventeenth century.

607. Arms of the canton of Basel-Stadt (the head of a bishop's crosier).

Furrier   Tailor   Painter   Captain of river craft   Carpenter

608. Arms of craftsmen etc. from Basel, fifteenth century.

113

HUNGARY

609. Arms of the Kingdom of Hungary, 1915.
Inescutcheon: dexter the original arms of Hungary proper, sinister later arms.
Principal shield: first quarter Dalmatia, second Croatia, third Slavonia, fourth
Transylvania (Siebenbürgen), fifth (an arm with a sword) Bosnia and Herzegovina,
sixth (an eagle on a rock) Fiume. Ensigned by the crown of St Stephen.

610. Arms of the Hungarian People's
Republic as it was from 1949 until
the Rising in 1956. After that time the
arms were changed once again to a
more traditional form.

611. The 'small coat of arms' of the
Kingdom of Hungary, 1916.

114

HUNGARY

612. City arms of Kecskemét.

613. City arms of Debrecen.

614. City arms of Budapest. The Communists added the red star to the original coat of arms in 1964.

615. Arms of the noble family of Harsányi, of which the writer Harsányi Zsolt (1887–1943) was a member. Severed heads of Turks are very common in Hungarian heraldry and are of course a reminder of the conflicts between the Hungarians and Turks that lasted for centuries.

616. City arms of Székesfehérvar.

617. Arms which Prince Sigismund Bathory of Transylvania granted to Captain John Smith in 1603.

619. Arms of the noble family of Chapi. Surrounding the shield is the badge of the Order of the Dragon. This, like Figs 618 and 621, is a coat of arms typical of the Hungarian nobility.

618. Arms of Simon von Kissolymos und Farczád.

620. City arms of Gyor.

621. Arms of the family of Bedö von Kalnock und Hodgya.

HUNGARY

622. Arms of the Hungarian national hero Prince Rákóczy Ferenc II (1676–1725), as used after 1711.

623. City arms of Szeged.

625. Arms of the Counts of Bethlen-Bethlen.

624. City arms of Esztergom.

PORTUGAL

626. The arms of Portugal. The shield is backed by an armillary sphere, an old nautical instrument.

627. Duke's coronet.

628. Pattern for a viscount.

629. Pattern for a baron.

630. Coronet of a marquis.

631. Pattern for nobility without title. In Portugal the coronet may rest on the helmet or the shield

632. Coronet of a count.

PORTUGAL

633. Arms of the capital Lisbon with the collar of the Order of the Tower and Sword. The provincial capitals also have a mural crown in gold. Other cities have a silver crown.

634. Arms of the country town of Arganil.

635. Arms of a province overseas: Goa, in India. (The waves in base should be shown white and green.)

SPANJ

636. Spain's royal crown.

637. Crown of the heir to the throne, the Prince of the Asturias.

638. Coronet of the Count of Barcelona.

639. The arms of Spain in modern times: first and fourth quarter, Castile quartered with León; second and third quarters, Aragon and Navarre; in base, the pomegranate of Granada (see also Fig. 271).

640. Coronet of the Count of Gerona.

641. Arms of the Spanish head of state, Francisco Franco.

642. Mural crown.

643. City arms of Madrid.

120

SPAIN

644. City arms of Valencia.

645. Arms granted to Christopher Columbus (c. 1446–1506) after the discovery of America. (From the *Crónica de Oviedo*, 1547.)

646. City arms of Barcelona.

647. Helmet and coronet for a prince of Castile.

648. Pattern for a marquis.

649. Helmet and coronet for a duke.

650. Pattern for a count.

651. Pattern for a viscount.

SPAIN

652. Pattern for a baron.

653. Pattern for a nobleman of ancient lineage, a *hidalgo*, who has no title.

654. Helmet for an *escudero*.

655. City arms of Soria. In Spanish heraldry a motto may be placed on the shield, but it is more common for it to be included in the bordure.

656. Helmet (facing sinister) for an illegitimate son (*bastardo*).

657. Arms of the province of León, based on those of the ancient kingdom of the same name.

658. Arms of the founder of the Order of Jesuits, Ignatius de Loyola (1491–1556).

659. City arms of Pamplona.

SPAIN

660. Arms of the poet and playwright
Lope de Vega Carpio (1562–1635).

661. Arms of the author of *Don
Quixote*, Miguel de Cervantes Saavedra
(1547–1616).

The bordure, often containing charges, is very common in Spanish heraldry, see also p. 163. Crests are rare, and nobility without title (who have no coronet to set on the helmet) often use ostrich feathers instead, usually in the same colours as the mantling, see above. Supporters may be used by all, but are nowadays rarely found.

662. Pattern for a marquis who is also
a grandee.

663. Pattern for a baron who is also a
grandee. See also Fig. 652.

'Grandee' is a special category within Spanish (Castilian) nobility and it can be combined with any other aristocratic rank. All grandees are entitled to a robe of estate with their coat of arms and they may rest their coronets directly on the shield, without a helmet.

BOHEMIA

664. The arms of Czechoslovakia since 1960.

665. Arms of the Bohemian Counts Radetzky, one of whom was the Austrian field marshal Josef Wenzel von Radetzky (1766–1858). (The handle of the spade should be brown.)

666. City arms of Prague.

667. The arms of Bohemia, fourteenth century.

668. The crown of the Bohemian St Wenceslas (Václas), fourteenth century. (All the jewels should be coloured.)

669. The arms of Moravia, fourteenth century.

ITALY

670. Arms of the former Italian heir to the throne (see also Fig. 370). The collar of the Order of the Annunciation surrounds the shield. Both this coat of arms and Figs 671 and 672 are variations of the white cross on a red field of the House of Savoy (see Fig. 206).

671. Arms of the Duke of Aosta.

672. Arms of the Duke of Genoa.

673. The iron crown of Lombardy which dates back to the ninth century.

674. The city arms of Rome.

675. The arms of the Italian Republic.

ITALY

676. The crown of the heir to the throne.

677. The Italian royal crown.

678. Crown for other princes.

679. Coronet for a duke of non-royal birth. See Fig. 696.

680. Coronet for a marquis. See also Fig. 699.

681. Coronet for a count. See also Fig. 682.

682. Coronet for a count. See also Fig. 681.

683. Coronet for a viscount.

684. Coronet for a baron. See also Fig. 685.

685. Coronet for a baron. See also Fig. 684.

686. Coronet for a nobleman without title (*nobile*).

687. Coronet for a patrician. See also Fig. 693.

688. Mural crown for boroughs.

689. Mural crown for large town.

ITALY

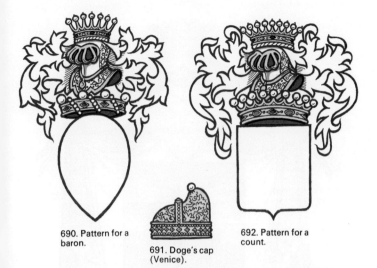

690. Pattern for a baron.

691. Doge's cap (Venice).

692. Pattern for a count.

Titled members of the Italian nobility can set their coronets on both shield and helmet, untitled noblemen, patricians and hereditary knights, only on the helmet. The Doge's cap (*corno dogale*) is used as a crest by Venetian families who descend from a doge.

693. Coronet for a patrician. See also Fig. 687.

695. Helm and coronet for a *nobile dei conti*.

694. Coronet for a prince (*principe*).

696. Arms of the ducal family of Diaz della Vittoria.

697. City arms
of La Spezia.

698. City arms
of Salerno.

699. Arms of the Marquises Marconi, the family of which the physicist and inventor of radio, Guglielmo Marconi (1874–1937), was a member.

700. City arms of Trieste.

701. City arms of Venice.

702. City arms of Pisa.

ITALY

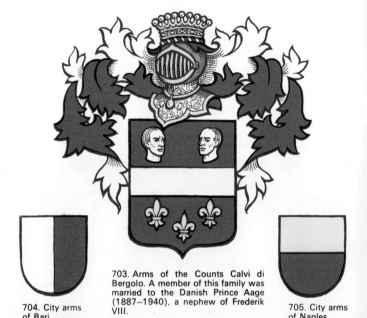

703. Arms of the Counts Calvi di Bergolo. A member of this family was married to the Danish Prince Aage (1887–1940), a nephew of Frederik VIII.

704. City arms of Bari.

705. City arms of Naples.

706. City arms of Ferrara.

708. City arms of Turin.

709. City arms of Florence.

707. City arms of Siena.

ITALY

710. Arms of the Barons Guariglia di Vituso.

711. Arms of the Viscounts Asquer di Fluminimaggiore.

712. Arms of a hereditary knight (*cavaliere ereditario*), in this case those of the Prunas family.

713. Arms of an Italian nobleman without title, in this case those of the Montini family. See also Fig. 879.

714. Arms of the patrician family of Segni, to which the former Italian president Antonio Segni (1962–4) belongs.

718. In Italian heraldry the chief of a shield often indicates a (former) political allegiance. A black double-headed eagle, or the upper part thereof, usually on a yellow field, signified allegiance to the Holy Roman Emperor. A blue chief with three yellow fleurs-de-lys beneath a red label showed the bearer to be a supporter of the Southern Italian King of Naples (see Fig. 699), originally a branch of the French Royal House. These two parties were also known as the Ghibellines and the Guelphs.

715. City arms of Genoa.

716. City arms of Messina.

717. City arms of Modena.

719. City arms of Pavia.

DENMARK

720. City arms
of Aarhus,
from c. 1250.

721. City arms
of Elsinore,
from the four-
teenth century.

723. The Danish Royal Arms, from
1948 to 1972.

722. Arms of Schleswig (South
Jutland) from 1245.

724. Arms of Greenland, from
the seventeenth century.

725. The city arms of
Copenhagen date back to
the thirteenth century.
This is the seventeenth-
century version.

726. The city arms
of Copenhagen in
a more recent form.

727. The arms of
Denmark go back to
the twelfth century.
They are included as
the first quarter in
Fig. 723.

134

DENMARK

728. Burchard von Ahlefeldt of Holstein was made a Danish count in 1672 and granted the above arms. The family coat of arms of the Ahlefeldts is the first quarter of the principal shield.

729. Holger Rosenkrantz was made Baron Rosenkrantz of Rosenlund in 1748 and granted the arms above. The family arms are on the inescutcheon.

730. The crown of the heir to the throne.

731. The king's crown.

732. Crown for younger princes.

733. Coronet for counts (see Fig. 728).

734. Coronet for barons (see Fig. 729).

735. Coronet for nobility without title.

736. Coronet for counts and barons.

737. Coronet for nobility without title.

The coronets were confirmed by the Danish King Christian V (1670–99). Figs 736 and 737 were intended as charges on the shield, but this decision was soon forgotten.

738. Arms of the non-aristocratic family of Hiort.

739. Arms of the non-aristocratic family of Arendrup.

741. City arms of Nyborg, from about 1300.

740. Arms of the Brahe family of ancient lineage.

742. Arms of the old aristocratic family of Holstein, of Ahlefeldt. See also Fig. 728.

DENMARK

743. The arms which Peter Wessel, the Danish naval hero, was granted when he was raised to the nobility in 1716 and given the name of Tordenskjold (thunderbolt). The first quarter illustrates the bearer's new name. The eagle in the second quarter signifies the battle in the previous year in which the Swedish frigate *Hvita örn* (white eagle) was taken. The cannon and three cannon balls in the third quarter symbolise the Danish signal of recognition which was three gunshots. The lion in the fourth quarter alludes both to the three lions in the coat of arms of Denmark and to the single lion in that of Norway.

744. City arms of Nexø, 1584.

745. Arms of the municipality of Linaa, 1947–70.

746. Arms of the municipality of Vamdrup, 1966–70.

NORWAY

747. The royal arms of Norway.

The lion can be traced back to the beginning of the thirteenth century. The attribute of St Olav's sainthood, the axe, was added about 1280. The collar of the Order of St Olav surrounds the shield.

748. The arms of Trygve Lie (1896–1968). The sword, the quill and the chairman's gavel symbolise various aspects of his life, among them his term of office as Secretary General of the United Nations.

750. The arms of Norway.

749. The arms of Olav Engelbrektson (1480–1538), the last Catholic archbishop of Norway. The second and third quarters contain his family coat of arms, the first and fourth, the arms of the archdiocese.

138

751. The arms of the violinist Ole Bull (1810—80). The charges on the shield are clearly allusive ('boles').

752. City arms of Oslo.

753. The arms of the composer Edvard Grieg (1843—1907). The family is said to be of Scottish origin.

754. The arms of the painter Erik Werenskiold (1855—1938), whose family belongs to the Dano-Norwegian aristocracy.

SWEDEN

755. The arms of Sweden, introduced by Albrecht of Mecklenburg (King of Sweden 1364—89) (see Fig. 209). The collar of the Order of the Seraphim surrounds the shield.

756. Arms of the province of Scania, ensigned with a ducal coronet, the equivalent of a royal title.

757. Arms of the province of Värmland, likewise ensigned with a ducal coronet.

758. Coronet for princes and princesses (ducal coronet).

759. Coronet of the heir to the throne.

SWEDEN

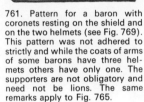

760. City arms of Stockholm.

761. Pattern for a baron with coronets resting on the shield and on the two helmets (see Fig. 769). This pattern was not adhered to strictly and while the coats of arms of some barons have three helmets others have only one. The supporters are not obligatory and need not be lions. The same remarks apply to Fig. 765.

762. City arms of Uppsala.

763. Pattern for nobility without title, with barred helmet.

764. Pattern for a person not of the nobility, with tournament helmet.

765. Pattern for the arms of counts (see Fig. 766). See also the caption to Fig. 761.

SWEDEN

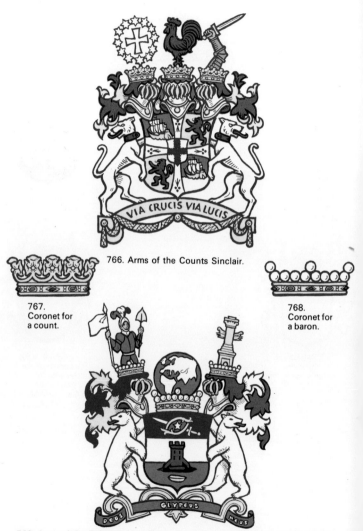

766. Arms of the Counts Sinclair.

767.
Coronet for
a count.

768.
Coronet for
a baron.

769. Arms of the Polar explorer Baron Adolf Erik Nordenskiöld (1832–1901).

SWEDEN

770. City arms of Ostersund.

771. Civic arms of Ragunda.

772. Arms of the aristocratic family of Hammarskjöld, ennobled 1610, to which the former Secretary General of the United Nations, Dag Hammarskjöld (1905–61), belonged.

773. Coronet for nobility without title (see also Fig. 230).

774. Mural crown as used in civic arms.

SWEDEN

775. The arms of the scientist and mystic Emmanuel Swedenborg (1688–1772), ennobled 1719.

776. Arms of a Knight of the Order of the Seraphim, the non-aristocratic Erik Boheman (born 1895), Leader of the Lower House of the Riksdag, the Swedish legislative assembly.

777. Arms of Archbishop Erling Eidem (born 1880). The rose and the fleur-de-lys are personal emblems, the red cross on white signifies his office.

778. Arms of the non-aristocratic family of Dahlerus.

779. Arms of the non-aristocratic family of Malmros.

780. Arms of the non-aristocratic family of Goos.

FINLAND

781. Arms of the province of Egentliga Finland.

782. The arms of Finland, which go back to the 1580s, a time when it was common for charges to have a symbolic meaning. The lion is defending himself with his straight (Western European) sword while stamping the curved (Russian) sabre underfoot.

783. Arms of the province of Savolax and for Kuopio län.

784. Arms of the capital, Helsinki.

785. City arms of Borgå.

786. Arms of the aristocratic family of Horn.

FINLAND

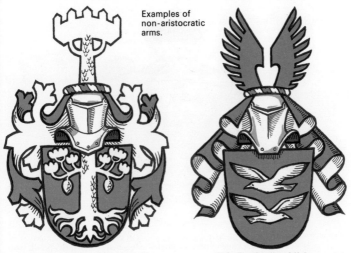

Examples of non-aristocratic arms.

787. The family of Honkajuuri.

788. The family of Kajava.

789. Arms of the rural district of Pungalaitio.

790. City arms of Vasa, decorated with the Cross of Liberty. (The background of the roundel in the centre of the Cross, containing the white rose, should be shown black.)

791. Arms of the rural district of Varpaisjarvi.

POLAND

792. Arms of the family of Radziwill, here as princes of the Holy Roman Empire. The shield in the centre is the family's original coat of arms, that of the Traby group (see opposite page).

793. City arms of Krakow.

794. City arms of Czestochowa.

795. The arms of Poland.

The white eagle on a red field goes back to the thirteenth century. The zig-zag bordure was used from 1918 by the president of the republic, but was done away with after the Second World War.

POLAND

796. Family coat of arms of the Counts Zamoyski which belongs to the Jelita group of arms.

797. Arms of the Marquises Wielopolski (-Gonzaga)-Myszkowski. The inescutcheon is the hereditary coat of arms belonging to the Staryikón group.

In Poland many noble families share as groups the same coat of arms (or *herb*), and such arms have (like all ancient arms of the Polish nobility) special names which differ from the names of the families. The names are often the same as the families' or groups' *proclamatio*, which is a sort of battle-cry.

798. City arms of Lodz, from the sixteenth century.

799. City arms of Przemysl, from the fourteenth century.

800. City arms of Lublin, from c. 1600.

POLAND

Ogonczyk

Oksza

Korczak

Lis

Szeliga

801. Six characteristic examples of the arms of related groups with their *proclamatio* names (see text p. 149).

Leliwa

802. Arms of the noble family of Dobrzycki, of the Leszczyc group. Noblemen usually bear the tournament helmet crowned with a coronet.

803. City arms of Warsaw, from the eighteenth century.

POLAND

Lodzia

Topór

Jastrzebiec-
Bolescicow

Sas

804. Five other typical coats of
arms of related groups with their
proclamatio names. (The tinctures
are not necessarily the same for all
families of a group.)

Rogala

805. Arms of the Barons Borowski,
belonging to the Jastrzebiec group.

151

RUSSIA

806. The crown of Ivan the Terrible, sixteenth century.

807. City arms of Kharkov, from the eighteenth century.

809. City arms of Jeka-terinoslav (from 1926: Dnjepro-petrovsk).

808. The 'small coat of arms' of Imperial Russia, as it looked in 1915. In the centre are the arms of Moscow (see Fig. 823) surrounded by the collar of the Order of St Andrew. The wings of the double-headed eagle are surmounted by the arms of cities and provinces. Dexter (*top to bottom*): Kazan, Poland (see Fig. 795), Taurida and Kiev (with Novgorod and Vladimir). Sinister: Astrakhan, Siberia, Georgia and Finland (see Fig. 782). The imperial crown at the top is taken from that of Catherine II, 1762. (The legs should be of the same colour as the beaks.)

810. City arms of Lvov, from the eighteenth century.

811. City arms of Minsk, from the sixteenth century.

RUSSIA

812. Helmets for Russian families with patents of nobility – in profile with visor raised.

813. Coronet for barons, after the French model, see Fig. 441.

814. Arms of the Princes Bariatinsky, who are descendents of the earliest known Russian ruler, Rurik (862–79).

815. Charges such as these are characteristic of old families of Tartar descent.

816. Arms of the Counts Tolstoi, one of whom was the writer Leo Tolstoi (1828–1910).

817. City arms of Rostov (on Don), 1811.

818. City arms of Novgorod, 1781.

819. City arms of Smolensk, 1780.

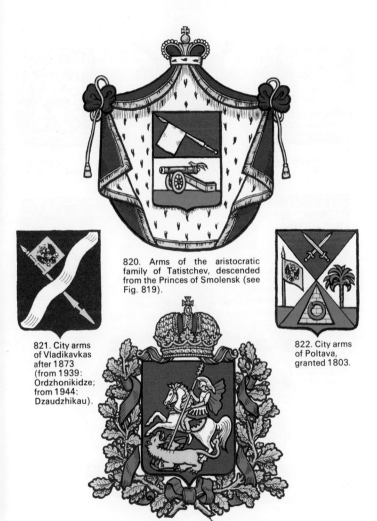

820. Arms of the aristocratic family of Tatistchev, descended from the Princes of Smolensk (see Fig. 819).

821. City arms of Vladikavkas after 1873 (from 1939: Ordzhonikidze; from 1944: Dzaudzhikau).

822. City arms of Poltava, granted 1803.

823. Arms of the 'Gouvernement' of Moscow, as they were in 1856.

RUSSIA

824. City arms of Kiev, 1782.*

825. City arms of St Petersburg (Leningrad), 1780.

826. City arms of Vladimir, 1781.

827. City arms of Tsaritsyn, 1857 (later Stalingrad, now Volgograd).

828. City arms of Kaluga, 1777.

*Sometimes shown with the sword red and the shield silver.

829. Coat of arms of the family of Rodzianko, typical of arms of the Ukrainian nobility.

830. Arms of the *leibkampanez* family of Simonev. The sinister half with sword is the family's own coat of arms. The dexter half is an augmentation (see p. 54). Peter the Great's daughter Elizabeth (1741–62) seized the Russian throne in 1741 by a coup d'état. The soldiers who had helped her were all raised to the nobility and were granted the same addition to the arms they already bore, or were presumed to bear: on a black field strewn with three stars a chevron with three grenades. They also all had the same crest – a grenadier's cap with plumes and wings – and were given the title of *leibkampanez*, meaning 'belonging to the company of Life Guards'.

831. City arms of Ufa, 1782.

832. City arms of Nijni-Novgorod (from 1932, Gorki), 1871.

157

RUSSIA

833. The arms of the Soviet Union.

After the establishment of the Soviet Union in 1917 this emblem was composed, contrary to former heraldic traditions, and has since then become the model for the arms of most other Communist countries (see below) and even for some non-Communist ones, such as the Republic of Italy, (see Fig. 675). The phrase 'Workers of the world unite' is printed in gold lettering on the ribbon in the fifteen official languages of the Soviet Union (now only fourteen).

834. Arms of the Russian Socialist Federal Soviet Republic.

835. Arms of the Estonian Socialist Soviet Republic.

All Soviet republics base their coat of arms on this pattern. A similar style is characteristic of the arms of East Germany (Fig. 493), Rumania, Jugoslavia and (until 1956) Hungary (Fig. 610) and, in Asia, the arms of the Chinese People's Republic (Fig. 16), the Mongolian People's Republic and North Korea. Bulgaria and Albania have retained their old coats of arms (a lion and a double-headed eagle respectively), but within a Soviet-inspired framework; Czechoslovakia has also retained its old lion, but with non-traditional accessories (Fig. 664). Of all the Communist states Poland is the only one to have kept its old coat of arms almost unchanged (see Fig. 795).

THE UNITED STATES

836. The arms of the United States from 1782.

837. Flag of the
state of Maryland,
1684.

838. Flag of the
state of Alaska,
1927.

839. Flag of the
state of Texas,
1839.

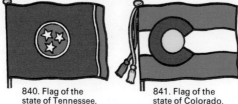

840. Flag of the
state of Tennessee,
1905.

841. Flag of the
state of Colorado,
1911.

THE UNITED STATES

842. Arms of the family of Washington, a member of which was the first president of the United States George Washington (1732–99), President 1789–97.

843. Arms of Princeton University, 1746.

844. Arms of the family of Franklin, one of whose members was Benjamin Franklin (1706–90).

845. Arms of the film actor Douglas Fairbanks jun. (born 1909).

846. Arms assumed by President Dwight D. Eisenhower (1890–1969). The crest alludes to his rank as a five-star general.

847. Arms of Morse College, part of Yale University, 1962.

848. Arms of Trumbull College, part of Yale University, 1933.

849. Arms of Yale University.

CANADA

850. Arms of Canada. Compare with Figs 309 and 424. (The mantling should be red lined with silver rather than the reverse, as shown here. The fringes of the banners are a decorative addition.)

851. Arms of the province of Ontario.

852. Arms of the province of Quebec. (The coat assigned in 1868 included only two fleurs-de-lys in chief and these were blue on gold.)

853. Arms of the provinc of British Columbia. (A gold antique crown shou be shown in the centre o the chief and three wavy blue bars are usually visible.)

854. The arms of Mexico. Assumed 1823, though the charges go back to Aztec mythology.

855. The arms of the Spaniard Francisco Montejo (c. 1473–1553), who conquered Yucatan.

856. Arms of the Spaniard Hernan (Fernando) Cortes (1485–1547), who conquered Mexico 1519–21.

857. Arms of Mexico City, granted by Charles V in 1523. See also the text on p. 123.

858. The arms of Brazil, assumed in 1889 when the country became a republic.

859. The arms of Chile, assumed 1834.

SOUTH AMERICA

859a. The Phrygian cap, a symbol of liberty that appears in various South American coats of arms, see e.g. Fig. 861.

860. Arms of Venezuela, assumed 1836.

861. Arms of Argentina, assumed 1813.

862. Arms of Peru, assumed 1825.

863. Arms of the Commonwealth of Australia, composed of the arms of the states of New South Wales, Victoria, Queensland, South Australia, Western Australia and Tasmania, assigned in 1912. (The mullets in the first quarter should have eight points and the stars in the second quarter should be silver; the swan in the fifth quarter is blazoned as 'naiant' and the compartment is sometimes decorated with golden wattle.)

864. Arms assigned to the Union of South Africa in 1910, combining the arms (now obsolete) of the provinces of Cape of Good Hope, Natal, Orange Free State and Transvaal. (The animals in the second quarter are blazoned as 'two Black Wildebeesten'.)

SOUTH AFRICA

865. Arms of the South African administered territory of South-West Africa, 1961.

866. Arms of the British Colony of Basutoland, 1951–66. (The wreath should be alternately gold and green, rather than green and gold.)

867. Arms of the province of Transvaal from 1955.

The palm and the sword are, like the coronet, symbols of secular authority.

868. Arms of Pope John XXIII.

869. Bishop's mitre, older form.

870. Pattern for an Anglican bishop (Durham). The crest-coronet is a special allusion to his former status as Count-Palatine.

871. Pattern for a German bishop (1487).

872. Pattern for a German bishop (c. 1500).

ECCLESIASTICAL HERALDRY

873. Arms of St Francis de Sales, 1657.

875. The triple papal crown, the tiara.

874. Arms of a patriarch in the Greek Orthodox church, Cardinal Gregorius Petrus XV Agagianian (died 1895). Behind the shield are the bishop's crosier, the staff of a patriarch, the cross of a patriarch and the rod of Aesculapius. Above is the mitre of an archbishop and below, the pallium.

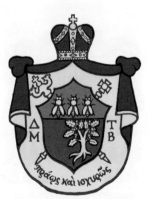

876. Arms of the Prior of Montpensier, fifteenth century. Behind the shield is the staff of a prior.

878. Arms of Demetrios, Metropolitan of Aleppo, Patriarch of the Greek Orthodox Church.

877. Pattern for a Swiss abbot, seventeenth century. Attached to the crosier is a *sudarium*.

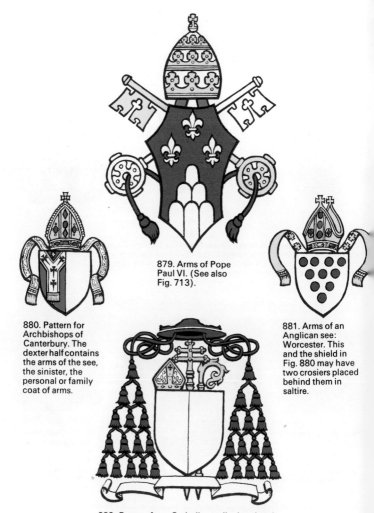

879. Arms of Pope Paul VI. (See also Fig. 713).

880. Pattern for Archbishops of Canterbury. The dexter half contains the arms of the see, the sinister, the personal or family coat of arms.

881. Arms of an Anglican see: Worcester. This and the shield in Fig. 880 may have two crosiers placed behind them in saltire.

882. Pattern for a Catholic cardinal and archbishop. The arms of the diocese and the personal arms are combined on the shield— cf. Fig. 880.

883. Arms of Francis, Cardinal Spellman, Archbishop of New York (died 1967). Dexter, the arms of the Archdiocese of New York, including the sails of a windmill, taken from the city arms of New York. Sinister, Cardinal Spellman's personal arms. The chief with the white cross on a red field is an augmentation (see p. 54), which shows he is a dignitary of the Order of Malta. This is also indicated by the cross of the Order behind the shield. Also behind the shield are the archiepiscopal staff and crosier, and resting on it is the archbishop's mitre. The achievement is ensigned by a red cardinal's hat.

Another papal emblem is the parasol, or *ombrellino* – see Figs 884 and 885.

884. The arms of the Italian Princes Odescalchi. The keys and the ombrellino above the shield indicate that a member of the family had been pope.

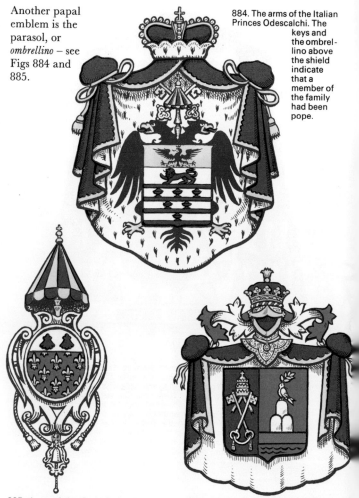

885. Arms of the Catholic basilica in St Louis, Missouri, U.S.A.

886. Arms of the Italian Princes Pacelli, one of whom was Pius XII.

ECCLESIASTICAL HERALDRY

887. Arms of Johann Egenolph von Knöringen, Bishop of Augsburg, sixteenth century.

888. Arms of Cardinal Carlo Carmelo de Vasconcellos Motta, Archbishop of Sao Paulo, Brazil.

890. Arms of Paul de Huyn, Catholic Patriarch of Alexandria. The chief of the shield and the cross of the Order behind it indicate that he is a senior dignitary of the Order of Malta.

889. Arms of the Catholic archbishop Philippe Bernardini. The cross of the Order of the Holy Sepulchre appears behind the shield.

891. Pattern for a Catholic bishop.

892. Arms of Henri-Charles du Cambout de Coislin (died 1732), Prince-Bishop of Metz.

893. Pattern for an abbot.

894. Pattern for an apostolic proto-notary.

895. Pattern for a papal chamberlain.

897. Pattern for a canon.

896. Pattern for the four highest prelates at the papal court who are called *di fiocchetto*.

898. Pattern for certain lesser dignitaries in the Catholic Church.

899. Arms of Pope Pius XII.

900. Pattern for
a Catholic priest.

901. Pattern for
an abbess.

902. Pattern for a prior.

175

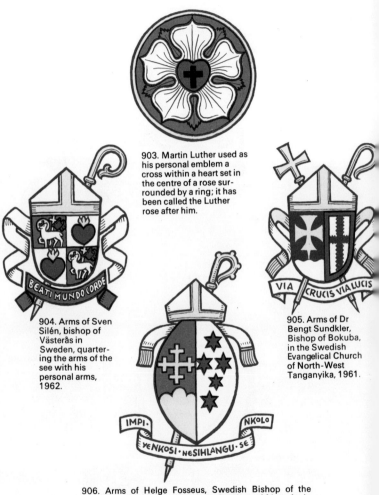

903. Martin Luther used as his personal emblem a cross within a heart set in the centre of a rose surrounded by a ring; it has been called the Luther rose after him.

904. Arms of Sven Silén, bishop of Västerås in Sweden, quartering the arms of the see with his personal arms, 1962.

905. Arms of Dr Bengt Sundkler, Bishop of Bokuba, in the Swedish Evangelical Church of North-West Tanganyika, 1961.

906. Arms of Helge Fosseus, Swedish Bishop of the Evangelical Lutheran Church in Southern Africa. As in Fig. 905 the bishop's personal arms are marshalled with those of the see. Note the African form of shield.

The Aims and Contents of the Book

Heraldry of the World is not a reference book on all coats of arms in existence. It contains less than a ten-thousandth, perhaps even less than a hundred-thousandth, of the arms to be found in the world. It might be better to call it a condensed heraldic dictionary containing characteristic examples of all important heraldic phenomena – characteristic, that is, both of the system itself (shield and helmet, charges, supporters etc.) and of each country's interpretation of it.

This latter is the important point. There are plenty of books on heraldry, in the principal languages especially, but most of them are written from a narrow, nationalist point of view dealing with the heraldry of only one country. What has been lacking is an international guide to heraldry, with a survey of the subject in all countries. Since no such book has appeared in recent years, the author decided to write and illustrate one himself. The result is the book you have in your hands.

One of the things that surprised the author when he came to grips with his undertaking was how great in fact the differences are in the heraldry of the various countries with regard to custom and usage, rules, style and taste, but this of course was only a further incentive to continue the work. Furthermore, heraldic art and style are in a constant process of development. The heraldic taste in Scandinavia nowadays has a clear leaning towards the abstract, while in Spain and Italy heraldry moves increasingly towards a naturalistic style. In Germany and France on the other hand traditional heraldry continues even now with its stylisation according to late Gothic and early Renaissance models.

In heraldic art it often happens that a few professional and popular heraldic artists influence, by their particular style, their own age, and posterity, to such an extent that the elements of it become characteristic of the nation to which they belong. In Germany this is particularly true of Albrecht Dürer (1471–1528), Hans Burgkmair (1474–1531) and Jost Amman (1539–91), the work of all of whom has been a great inspiration to the author of this book. But since the aim is not to show the best artistic examples of coats of arms but rather those most typical of a nation or an epoch, the author has deliberately not followed his own personal taste but has tried to copy characteristic models as closely as possible.

A nation's heraldry reflects its historical and cultural development. Throughout the history of Europe, from the beginnings of heraldry up to our own times, national frontiers have shifted time and again, often as the result of war, but also for example through marriage or inheritance. And when a country increased its territory or its influence in some other way, its heraldry as a rule followed suit. This is the reason for indications of German, French and Spanish heraldry found in Italy side by side with the various forms of its native heraldry. This again is of course the basis for colonial heraldry and its special differences. One exception is the complicated heraldic system thought up by Napoleon which did not survive him. Families and towns with a Napoleonic coat of arms have as a rule adapted this later to be more in keeping with their homeland's time-honoured heraldry.

The French Revolution from 1789 onwards abolished not only the lilies of the royal house but also all other French coats of arms, only to introduce its own system of emblems and symbols. In presentation these differed considerably from the traditional and were really just a new form of heraldry. Something similar occurred in North America after the War of Independence, 1776–83, and in South America after the break-away from Spain at the beginning of the nineteenth century. Although some leaders of the North American revolution possessed coats of arms and used them, as in the case of George Washington and Benjamin Franklin, it was gradually considered undemocratic and snobbish to bear arms in the United States. The bearings which were devised for constituent states or cities rarely had any similarity to traditional arms and are called 'seals'.

Latin America's heraldry also diverged from the well-established European standard, but this was not only for political reasons. Most national emblems in South and Central America were created at a time when heraldry as an art form was not of consequence anywhere in the world. Some of them can hardly be called coats of arms at all.

Canada is an exception. Its long association with Great Britain, first as a colony and later as a member of the British Commonwealth, resulted in British customs and usages with regard to heraldry being followed.

In Communist countries from East Germany to China, following the revolution in Russia in 1917 and even more so after the Second World War, a completely new and rather uniform series of state emblems has developed which in their presentation differ completely from the earlier arms of these states. Yet on the other hand traditional heraldry flourishes in many new and to some extent revolutionary states, as for example in Africa.

Thus heraldry is in fact an international phenomenon, but it has very characteristic national and political differences. And that is what this book sets out to demonstrate.

Some readers may think it strange to find so many symbols of nobility, such as coronets and the like, in a modern book on heraldry. But we must not forget that heraldry in its origins is an aristocratic phenomenon and that such symbols are a part of its history.

The Origins of Heraldry (p. 7)

The origin of heraldry among warriors as a form of decoration for their equipment is reflected in the two meanings of the word 'arm'. To differentiate between these two expressions the plural form 'arms' is used in heraldry. The arm of the warrior is his sword or lance, his arms are his emblems. There is a similar connection in other languages too. The German *Waffen* refers to a weapon for offence or defence, *Wappen* refers to his coat of arms. The expression 'coat of arms' actually originated in the surcoat bearing an emblem which the warrior wore over his hauberk (see Fig. 34).

The Origins of Heraldry; Heraldic Charges (pp. 7-8)

Armorial bearings of cities mostly fall into seven categories relating to their origins. Many city arms show the city itself or a dominant part of it: the city wall, the gate, a castle, church, bridge or tower.

In another large group, the arms include a figure representing the city's patron saint or the saint's attribute. Other armorial bearings reflect the city's livelihood, its most important product or export. Hence we find herrings, bales of wool, bunches of grapes etc. or, more recently, two crossed pencils, the wheels of a locomotive, or the two crossed shrimps of Christianshaab in Greenland, a symbol of the city's canning industry.

Related to the above are city coats of arms which have developed from the seal or device of the city's most important craft guild or from that of some other trade organisation. One example is the coat of arms of Paris (Fig. 429). The captains of river craft played a dominant role in the city in the Middle Ages, and the device in their guild's seal and the emblem of the guild were gradually (in combination with the royal lilies) accepted as the bearings of the city itself.

Some city arms can be traced back to military standards or banners used by the citizens in battle or in defence of their city. This is true of a number of cities and cantons in Switzerland (see pp. 112 and 113).

Some ancient towns, particularly in Germany and England, have armorial bearings which are identical with, or a variation of, those of the prince or nobleman on whose land they were built and whose protection they enjoyed. A Danish example is Naestved, built on land owned by the Catholic Church, which includes the papal emblem, two crossed keys (see Fig. 879) in its coat of arms.

Finally there is a large group of civic arms which are allusive, i.e. containing a charge which makes a play on the name of the town (see also page 34). The city of Lille has a lily, the city of München (Munich), a monk (German: *Mönch*), and so on.

When councillors or other burghers assumed coats of arms, they were often inspired by the arms of their city which in this way were continued in many variations as well as in their original form.

Heraldic Charges; New Usages and Forms (pp. 8 and 10)

'Herald' is a general term for three classes or offices, 'kings of arms', 'heralds' and 'pursuivants' (meaning those who follow). The individual offices might be named after the arms of the prince concerned (which the heralds wore on their tabards, see Fig. 13) or of one of his estates, or then again after an order of which he was the head. The King of Arms of Scotland is thus called Lyon (lion), after the arms of Scotland. Several of the Kings of Arms of the Holy Roman Empire of German Nation bore the title Romreich. The highest in the hierarchy of England's kings of arms is called Garter King of Arms, after the Order of the Garter. Among the titles of the Danish mediaeval heralds are the names Zealand and Jutland.

The Legal Aspect of Heraldry

Who is entitled to armorial bearings? The answer is that, with certain local limitations (which will be mentioned when individual countries are dealt with), everybody has the right to bear arms. This is how it was at the very beginnings of heraldry in the Middle Ages, and so it is today.

The first bearings were independently assumed, and so are many nowadays. But from about 1400 kings started to grant patents of arms, both to individuals (sometimes, but not always, in connection with ennoblement) and to towns and corporations. Such titles to arms bestowed by the king were regarded as superior to those adopted independently, and this led to the king's being requested either to grant new arms or to recognise previously assumed arms. Many were only too glad to pay for such a patent of arms or recognition of arms, and thus the granting or straightforward sale of patents of arms became in many countries a good source of revenue for the king or for those officers to whom he had entrusted jurisdiction in matters of heraldry.

In some countries, particularly Great Britain, the heralds decided that a coat of arms that had been assumed independently and without ratification was not valid and that the only legal way of claiming a right to bear arms was to request it from the heralds appointed by the sovereign. This viewpoint is held officially in Great Britain today, but is less widely held on the Continent.

Some British heraldists consider that a grant of arms confers a certain kind of nobility. There is in fact no creation of untitled nobility in England, but an 'armiger' ranks as a gentleman, a degree which can be regarded in all but name as a form of lesser nobility: and a grant of arms, which can be withheld from applicants deemed unsuitable, has long served as a form of recognition of social status. In Scotland all arms are considered to be 'ensigns of nobility'.

A coat of arms is inherited largely in the same way as a name is inherited. Children as a rule bear their father's arms, but if the mother is of a higher rank they sometimes choose to assume her coat of arms. In Spain and Portugal children can inherit the arms of both father and mother, and when a woman marries she assumes her husband's bearings combined in some cases with those of her father (or mother). In Great Britain and Western Europe during the Middle Ages it was customary among the aristocracy for every male member of a family to add a charge (a 'difference' or 'brizure' or 'cadency' mark) to the family arms, or to alter the tinctures, so that no two men of the same family bore arms that were exactly the same (see, e.g., p. 85). In Scotland an attempt has been made to enforce this system (see p. 72) and it is practised within the royal family. Both male and female members all use a small addition to the royal arms – a 'label' charged with roses, anchors, crosses etc. – which distinguishes their arms from those of the other princes and princesses and from those of the sovereign. However, these marks are assigned specially in each case and do not follow the normal rules of cadency.

It is one thing to have the right to bear arms, but quite another to bear a specific coat of arms. The original and most important purpose of heraldry was and is identification, and this implies the principle that all coats of arms should differ. From the Middle Ages and the Renaissance we have reports of lawsuits, in which a person who had by chance assumed arms that were already borne by another was compelled by law to adopt a new coat of arms that could not be confused with the first. For heraldic legislation, legal protection, etc., see the various countries.

Shield and Helmet (pp. 11–22)

A warrior could put his emblem on all parts of his equipment (see Fig. 34), but the shield with its large solid surface was the best suited. It was usually made of wood covered with leather or parchment (sometimes covered in canvas above this) on which the device was painted. The emblem could also be embossed in low relief in the leather itself or picked out in metal studs.

When in use as defence, the shield was carried on the left arm, supported by straps at the back of the shield. When not in use it hung at the left side by a strap over the right shoulder. Throughout the whole of the Middle Ages it was common to show a coat of arms in a slanting position, just as it must have looked hanging at the warrior's left side (see, e.g., Fig. 22 and p. 17). Occasionally it was depicted suspended by its strap and hanging from a tree.

The earliest form of shield in heraldry was the elongated, kite-shaped Norman shield (see Figs 31 and 33). Examples have been found on seals from the twelfth century and from an enamelled and engraved tomb plate which shows Geoffrey Plantagenet (of Anjou) with gold lions on a blue shield. According to a contemporary chronicle he was granted this coat of arms by Henry I of England when he was knighted in 1127.

Heraldry however followed the changes in style and fashion, and this is reflected in the varying forms of shield (see pp. 13 and 14). In the seventeenth and eighteenth centuries particularly, during the periods of the Baroque and the Rococo, when the shield was no longer used for practical purposes but was merely continued in graphic form, decorative and distorted shapes far removed from a shield's original function were invented. The heraldic artist of our time must for each occasion consider seriously which form of shield he intends to use and should make it a rule from the aesthetic point of view especially to base his work on the early forms of heraldry in preference to the second-hand heraldry of later times. The same is of course true for the helmet and other heraldic appurtenances.

The helmet too has taken on different forms in different periods. The oldest type in heraldry is the barrel helm, also called the great helm (see p. 15). It was worn with a hauberk which also covered the neck and head of the warrior, and it was by degrees furnished with horns and other embellishments (see Fig. 36). When the warrior was not fighting, the helmet usually hung at his saddle.

The good heraldic artist does not mix elements of different styles, and a barrel helm should therefore be used only with the forms of shield and mantling which belong to the same period, i.e. the thirteenth and fourteenth centuries. For the same reason the coronet should not be used together with the barrel helm.

Around 1400 the barrel helm was replaced by the tournament helmet (see p. 16) and in the course of the century this again by the barred helmet (see p. 18). In Spain, Italy and France the number of bars indicated the bearer's rank. Around the neck-piece of the barred helmet there often hangs a chain or a ribbon with a medallion. A variation of this type of helmet has the bars replaced with a grating or lattice-work of metal wire.

The visored helmet became popular in the sixteenth century and is still used in certain countries with the visor either open or closed (pp. 19 and 20). In Central Europe, Germany and Scandinavia, however, it seems to have fallen out of use completely.

In some countries the position of the helmet indicates the rank of the bearer. In England the golden helmet of the royal arms and the helmet in the arms of a baronet or knight must be shown *en face* (see Figs 48 and 225), while all other ranks show the helmet in profile (facing dexter). In France, Spain and Italy a helmet shown *en face* indicates the highest ranks, from marquis upwards. Most other countries attach no importance to the position of the helmet, the crest being the determining factor. The inside of the helmet is usually red, but may also be of another colour, when for example it corresponds with the field of the shield.

During the centuries the mantling of the helmet has become one of heraldry's most decorative effects (see pp. 11–22) and to exclude it when a coat of arms includes a helmet is considered incorrect heraldry. The details of the mantling's shape depend on the position and proportions of the coat of arms and on the desire of the artist, but in every instance some part of both sides of the mantling must be shown. Its tinctures are as a rule the same as the shield's, the most important 'colour' being on the outside and the most important 'metal' on the inside – though there are many exceptions.

Tinctures, Divisions and Charges (pp. 23–33)

The oldest escutcheons were as a rule very simple and bore only two tinctures, a 'colour' and a 'metal'. The charges were chosen and designed as simply as possible, since the purpose of the device was to be recognised and identified, even at a distance. For this reason most of the oldest family coats of arms are uncomplicated in design, in contrast with the majority of the arms which have been designed since the

Renaissance (see pp. 51, 110, 137).

In many cases however the original simple beauty of the coat of arms has been marred by the marshalling of several devices on a single shield or by augmentations (see p. 54). Ruling princes often combined on the same shield their family arms with the arms of the countries or territories where they held sway, or even of countries they did not possess but merely considered they had a right to, or had once had a right to (until 1801 the royal arms of Great Britain contained the lilies of France, which had been included as a quartering since 1340. The three crowns of Sweden are still included in the Danish royal arms, p. 134). Such divided and redivided shields were copied by people not of royal birth who believed that many divisions in a shield indicated noble ancestry. In the end coats of arms were often composed of several divisions from the very start (pp. 109 and 110). As an example of this nearly all the arms of Swedish counts included quarterings and an inescutcheon (Fig. 766).

The simplest coats consist merely of a shield divided up by one or more lines into fields of two or more different tinctures. The most important divisions and lines are shown on pp. 24–26 but the possibilities are virtually limitless. Each different charge can be further varied by the tinctures used. With merely two tinctures in a coat of arms it is possible to combine the two 'metals' silver and gold and the four 'colours' red, blue, black and green in sixteen different ways. Charges based on the commoner divisional lines are called honourable ordinaries and have their own names: the chief, the bar, the pale, the bend, the chevron, the canton, the flaunches etc. (see pp. 24 and 25). The eight divisions as shown on p. 26, Figs 77 and 80, also have their own concise terminology. (Fig. 77: lozengy, checky, chevrony, paly. Fig. 80: paly bendy, barry bendy, barry parted per pale, dancetty).

The tinctures of heraldry include the colours red, blue, black, green and sometimes, but rarely, purple, and the metals silver and gold. For convenience, white may be substituted for silver and yellow for gold (see also p. 207). In heraldry of a more recent date it is also possible to meet with charges in 'proper' colours, as for example a flesh-coloured arm.

There are as well a number of patterns called 'furs', ermine and miniver or vair being the most usual (see p. 23). The black tufts in ermine can be combined in various ways; they represent the black tails of the ermine or stoat. The white and blue fields in vair are probably a stylised version of the light-coloured fur on the belly of the grey sqirrel and the darker fur on its back. These patterns in fur probably go back to shields which in the infancy of heraldry were covered with real fur. See also Figs 293 and 466.

As far as tinctures in heraldry are concerned the rule is that colour should not be superimposed on colour, but only on metal, and vice versa (see p. 23). But there are some exceptions. The rule is for example not applicable to details such as the claws of animals, hoofs, horns, tongues etc. Fur is 'amphibious' and may be superimposed on either colour or metal. On occasions the rule is deliberately broken, the best known example being the shield of the Crusaders' Kingdom of Jerusalem: on a field argent a cross potent between four plain crosslets or. But that there is some sense in the rule can be seen e.g. from the arms of the city of Bonn (Fig. 529), in which the red lion on a blue field is much less distinct and aesthetically pleasing than it would have been if the rule had been regarded. See also Figs 588 and 622.

The distinction between certain divisions and certain ordinaries (p. 24) may seem a little involved. If for example a shield is divided twice vertically and the outer areas of the fields are of the same tincture, the field in the middle is called a 'pale' and the whole is described for example as 'on a field argent a pale sable' (Fig. 67c). If the outer areas are of different tinctures, the middle figure is not necessarily considered an independent charge but the shield can be described as being 'tierced in pale' (divided twice vertically into three separate sections) (Fig. 66b, second example).

The cross (p. 25) is one of the most common charges in heraldry and is used in many different forms, only a selection being shown in this book. A plain, simple cross is found frequently in Italian municipal heraldry; some examples can be seen on p. 133. The famous eight-pointed Maltese cross occurs in the achievement of the Order of Malta (Fig. 278) and appears behind the shield, in the crown, and hanging from the chain beneath. It can also be seen in the municipal arms of localities which were once possessions of the Order or in which some of its properties were situated, as in the arms of Neukölln, Fig. 522. The coat of arms of Switzerland is a white Greek cross on a red field (Fig. 593). The principal shield of the Swedish royal house is divided into four quarters by a yellow cross, and the Danish royal arms by the cross of the Order of the Dannebrog (Fig. 723).

Practically anything that can be depicted can be used as a heraldic charge. The possibilities are so extensive that pp. 27-33 can only show a few characteristic examples: human and anthropomorphic figures, fabulous beasts, animals of all kinds, buildings, weapons and implements, flowers and trees, and so on, as well as parts of all these such as

185

heads, wings, leaves, wheels and so on. And these relatively few examples themselves would be far too numerous to describe in detail within the limits of this book, so descriptions of a few of the most important must suffice.

In heraldry as elsewhere the lion is the king of beasts (pp. 27 and 28). At the dawn of heraldry large numbers of princes took a lion, or more than one, as their emblem – such as the King of Leon (Fig. 657), the Kings of England and Scotland (Fig. 309), the King of Denmark (Fig. 727), the King of Sweden, the King of Norway (Fig. 747) and the King of Bohemia (Fig. 667) – and later their example was followed by other princes or states (see the Netherlands (Fig. 387), Belgium (Fig. 415) and Finland (Fig. 782)), as well as by knights, burghers and towns throughout the whole of Europe. The lion is also very common as a supporter.

The lion is as a rule shown rampant (see Figs 87 and 96), but frequently also passant (Fig. 84). When a lion passant is shown with its head facing the observer, or *en face*, it is sometimes called a leopard. This term has however led to many misconceptions and therefore most modern heraldists avoid it. The other positions illustrated on pp. 27–8 are all fairly rare.

The lion with two tails, or with its tail divided in two, occurs quite frequently. It is usual, but not necessary, to colour the tongue and claws differently from the rest of the body. Many lions are crowned or wear a collar, at times with a chain, or hold something in their front paws such as a sword, an axe or a wheel. In England the lion may even have a crown around its neck. All this goes for other animals as well.

The antlers of the hart or stag are referred to as 'attires' (or in Scottish heraldry as 'tynes') : the stag is 'attired' when bearing antlers (Fig. 137).

In the same way as the lion is predominant among animals, the eagle is so among birds (see pp. 27 and 28). The eagle is usually shown stylised, seen from the front with outstretched wings, but with the head in profile, as in Fig. 83. A more recent representation is to be found in Napoleon's coat of arms as emperor (Fig. 467). An eagle with two heads is called a double-headed eagle (Fig. 92); in this form it was the favourite heraldic beast of emperors. A double-headed eagle formed the basis of the arms of Imperial Russia (see Fig. 808) and was also the device of the old German emperors from 1410 (p. 7). After the fall of the Holy Roman Empire in 1806, the Habsburg emperors of Austria assumed the double-headed eagle until 1918 (Fig. 567). The German Empire from 1870 had an ordinary eagle with only one head in its arms

(Fig. 492), and Western Germany (Fig. 494) and the Republic of Austria (Fig. 570) have one now.

The best known heraldic flower is the lily, known as the fleur-de-lys, a stylised lily or iris (see Fig. 133). It was the emblem of the French kings (pp. 82 and 85) but is not specifically French and is known all over Europe. A single heraldic lily may be borne, or the field may be 'semy de lys' when lilies are strewn over the shield as the French king originally bore them (see Figs 447 and 429); or the lily may be combined with other charges (Figs 73, 76, and 363). In England the lily is also used as a mark of cadency for the sixth son (see Fig. 370). A garden lily is sometimes used in heraldry, though only rarely. In the arms of Eton, the famous public school, the heraldic lily and the natural lily both occur (see Fig. 308).

In England especially the rose is used quite frequently. In the Middle Ages a red and a white rose were the badges of the two lines of the English royal house called Lancaster and York, and after the Wars of the Roses these two emblems were united to form what is called the Tudor rose (see Fig. 261). In England a rose is also a mark of cadency for the seventh son (Fig. 370). Another famous rose emblem is the Luther rose (see Fig. 903).

The heraldic sun (Fig. 148) has rays which are usually depicted alternately straight and wavy. It is occasionally shown with a human face. The same is true of the crescent or half-moon (Figs 149, 150, 152 and 153). In England a crescent is the mark of a second son (see Fig. 370). Stars have either five, six, seven or eight points (Fig. 154). A star with wavy points (Fig. 161) occurs frequently in English heraldry and is known as an 'estoile'. Also common is a plain star or 'mullet' which is used as the cadency mark of a third son. When pierced with a hole it may be described as a 'spur rowel'.

The scallop shell (Fig. 105) is very common. In the Middle Ages this type of shell was used as a kind of certificate for pilgrims who had visited the tomb of St James of Compostela in Northern Spain, and thus became the attribute of this saint and also a general symbol of pilgrimage. In Denmark the name James became Ib (for Iacobus) and in Danish heraldry the scallop shell is often called an ibskål ('Ib shell').

Another common charge is the castle (Fig. 126), usually shown as two fortified towers joined by a wall. There may be a gate in the wall, open or closed, with a portcullis. A tower by itself is also frequently used. It is at times surmounted by three smaller towers (see example Fig. 271), and in this case it is difficult to decide whether it is a tower or a castle. There are however many other varieties of castle-like buildings, especially in civic heraldry – cf. the arms of the City of Edinburgh (Fig. 348), Antwerp (Fig. 421), Budapest (Fig. 614), Copenhagen (Fig. 725) and Mexico (Fig. 857).

There are many versions of ships and boats, from Viking ships and other forms of sailing ship to the steam and motor ships of the present day. Examples can be seen in Figs 366, 429 and 633.

Trees, growing or uprooted and showing roots (see Figs 130 and 132), as well as their leaves, are very common. The oak seems to be the most popular, but we also come across the lime, the spruce and the pine and sometimes the palm too. In the former arms of South Africa the third quarter contains an orange tree, an allusive charge for the Orange Free State (see Fig. 864).

Saints and apostles occur, especially in civic heraldry, e.g. in the arms of Brussels, which show probably the archangel Michael (Fig. 417); Trier, the apostle Peter (Fig. 534); and Kiev, the archangel Michael again, (Fig. 824). The arms of Moscow show St George killing the dragon (Figs 808 and 823), an allusion to the defeat of the Tartars by Dmitri Donskoi (A.D. 350–89), Grand Duke of Moscow and Vladimir.

All these and other figures can be placed and combined in an un-quartered shield and in all the various sections and heraldic quarterings into which a shield may be partitioned. See for example the arms of the family of von Borsig (Fig. 212); of Karl Maria von Weber and Sven Hedin (Figs 229 and 230); of Benjamin Disraeli (Fig. 305); and of the cities of Kaiserslautern and Koblenz (Figs 532 and 533).

Arms of Alliance and Women's Coats of Arms (pp. 42-4)

A person who, perhaps because of his possessions, had the right to several coats of arms originally bore each on its own shield, but the shields were often, as for example on his seal, grouped to produce a decorative effect. In more recent heraldry we find such a grouping of individual arms all belonging to the same person in the coat of the Russian Czars where the eagle has several shields displayed on each wing (see Fig. 808). It could also happen that a knight who was entitled to three coats of arms bore one on his shield, the other on his banner and the third on his horse's caparison.

At the close of the twelfth century the custom had already started of combining two or more coats of arms on the same shield. The oldest procedure was to divide in half vertically each of the escutcheons to be combined, the dexter half of one and the sinister half of the other, and join them to form a new coat of arms. The result of such dimidiation might however not only be unsightly but could be entirely incorrect. If a coat of arms containing a chevron is dimidiated, the result is one half with a charge which is in fact a bend (see Fig. 67), and this is unsuitable, since it might be another family's arms. So whole coats of arms were combined instead, usually in a vertically divided shield. But this was not a very successful method either, because the proportions of the original escutcheon were spoilt. In Spain in the first half of the thirteenth century a way out of all these problems was found, and in the following centuries it was adopted all over Europe.

This was the system known as quartering. The shield was divided vertically and horizontally into four parts, all of which had more or less the same proportions as the original shield. If only two coats of arms are to be combined, they can both appear twice, the most important, often the paternal one, being placed in the first and fourth quarters, the other in the second and third (Fig. 366). Three coats are placed with the most important in the first and fourth quarters, the two others in the second and third (Fig. 309). Four coats are set each in their own quarter (Figs 2 and 291). If necessary a shield can be divided into even more 'quarters', six, nine or whatever number is required (Fig. 575). And each of the quarterings can itself be quartered (Fig. 271), and so on.

Another way of combining two coats of arms is to place one within the other as an inescutcheon. In Great Britain this is done according to strict rules, e.g. by a man whose wife personally bears a title of nobility (Fig. 240), or whose wife is an heraldic heiress (i.e. has no surving brothers or nephews to carry on her paternal arms). The children of such a marriage can quarter the arms of their father and mother (Fig. 234). On the Continent the inescutcheon is used almost exclusively in connection with quarterly coats and usually contains the person's or family's original or most important coat of arms (Figs 415, 580 and 609). Sometimes the inescutcheon contains a symbol of office (Fig. 288) or an augmentation (Fig. 282).

The chief too can be used in the combination of two coats of arms on one shield (Figs 244 and 718).

Archbishops, bishops and abbots can combine the arms of their see or monastery with their personal arms, either by placing them side by side (Figs 237 and 883) or by quartering (Figs 749 and 904). The arms of office are placed in the first, or the first and fourth, quarters and the personal or family arms in the second (or second and third). A married man can combine his own arms with those of his wife or, in specific cases, with the arms of his office or an order of knighthood, but he cannot do both at the same time.

A woman inherits her father's arms undifferenced. Some heraldists are of the opinion that women are not entitled to bear a helmet and crest, but this is a theory which is not everywhere accepted. In France, the Netherlands and Great Britain a woman's shield is often lozenge-shaped (pp. 44 and 53). This form of shield is known from the thirteenth century and was then used by men as well, but during the course of the sixteenth century it became the custom for women only to use it. But in Western Europe not all coats of arms for women took on this form, and in Germany and Scandinavia it never caught on. This is no doubt connected with the fact that the lozenge shape completely distorts the accepted heraldic proportions; certain devices, particularly when quartered, are almost impossible to reproduce in this form. The oval, which is also sometimes used for the arms of women (Fig. 247), is considerably better.

A husband's and wife's arms may be marshalled on one shield, as shown on pp. 42–3. On the Continent the husband bears only his own personal coat of arms though the arms of man and wife can also be combined each in its own shield (see Figs 232 and 235). The husband's arms, which are placed on the dexter, are often *de courtoisie* turned towards the sinister to 'respect' the wife's.

In the heraldry of England and Scotland there are a number of rules for the combination of the arms of married couples, including those relating to their respective ranks. Some examples are given on pp. 43–4, but the circumstances are so specific that we cannot go into details here.

The Special Features of Heraldry in Various Countries

In heraldry, as in painting and architecture, one can distinguish not merely what is characteristic of certain epochs but also what is typical in style for the various nations. In some countries there was a predilection for a certain form of shield, a certain type of helmet and certain specific devices; in other countries for a different shield, different helmet and different devices. And the depiction of the same devices can vary from country to country. An eagle was not portrayed in England in the same way as it was in Germany. In this manner a number of national features developed.

In spite of the fact that heraldry contains the same basic elements everywhere, one is aware of a distinct historical and cultural atmosphere when one compares for example the arms of a Spanish *hidalgo* (Figs 660 and 661) with a comparable Hungarian coat of arms (Figs 618, 619 and 621), or the arms of a British knight (Fig. 329) with those of a

Polish nobleman (Figs 801 and 802). French heraldry, taking the city arms of Rouen and Limoges (Figs 455 and 457) as examples, seems often to reflect the country's history under the Bourbon kings and the influence of the Roman Church, while Russian arms (Figs 815 and 829) bring to mind the armies of knights who fought the Mongols on the steppes of Russia. And does not the histrionic classicism of Napoleonic heraldry (pp. 90–3) remind us of the imperial generals and the imperial guards in their ostentatious uniforms?

In the following pages an attempt is made with the help of the corresponding coloured plates to describe and give examples of the heraldic characteristics of the various countries in their modern form.

Great Britain and Ireland (pp. 60–75)

Great Britain differs from other countries in that there are heraldic officers who still perform their function, and heraldic regulations which still pertain. This latter is particularly true of Scotland. The heraldic authorities hold the view that no coat of arms can be assumed as a matter of course; it must be assigned or be confirmed by them. Some heraldists insist that a legally granted coat of arms endows the bearer with a form of nobility, but this is not generally accepted (see p. 181). The College of Arms controls England's heraldic administration. At its head is the Earl Marshal, an office which is hereditary in the family of the Dukes of Norfolk (Fig. 291). The most important of the heraldic officials proper is Garter King of Arms (see p. 180). In Scotland Lord Lyon King of Arms (his name is taken from the royal arms of Scotland) is the highest heraldic authority. His is a royal appointment and he himself appoints the other Scottish heralds and pursuivants (see p. 180). In England all kings of arms, heralds and pursuivants are appointed by the reigning sovereign. Ulster King of Arms formerly had authority over the whole of Ireland. Now his jurisdiction is limited to Northern Ireland (the office being combined with that of Norroy King of Arms), while the Republic of Ireland (Eire) has its own Chief Herald of Ireland.

Another thing particular to Britain is the title of baronet which ranks below the peerage. A baronet inherits the title of Sir, in contrast to a knight, who only holds this title during his own lifetime. Baronets and knights bear the same characteristic helmet in their arms: set affronty with raised visor (see Figs 48, 318, 327 and 329). The rank of baronet was introduced in 1611 by King James I in connection with the conquest and colonisation of Ulster, and this is why the arms of baronets (other than those of Nova Scotia) include a small shield with a red hand on a white field (Figs 330, 331 and 332), derived from the coat of arms of Ulster (see Fig. 375). From 1625 certain Scottish baronets were given the attribute 'of Novia Scotia' in connection with the colonisation of this region on Canada's Atlantic coast (see Fig. 364).

Helmets are used according to strict rules. The royal helmet, borne by Queen Elizabeth and the royal princes, is a barred helmet in gold, set affronty (Fig. 225). Peers bear silver or steel-coloured barred helmets with gold ornamentation, in profile, so that five bars can be seen (Figs 57, 272, 313, 322 and 328). The helmets of baronets and knights have already been mentioned. On the first rung of the ladder of rank is the gentleman or esquire (the two ranks were previously distinct and to some extent still are), who bears a steel-coloured tournament helm, set in profile (see Figs 333, 337, 338, 376, 385 and 386). Formerly a visored helmet was often used as shown on p. 19, but nowadays the jousting helm without visor is generally preferred.

The inside of a helmet is usually red but may be of other colours. If there are two or more helmets they generally face the same way, i.e. to the dexter (see Fig. 57), not towards one another as is the style on the Continent. The rule about the position of the helmet – in profile or *en face* – depends on the owner's rank and often makes it difficult for the heraldic artist to make sense of a coat of arms: a baronet's helmet should be depicted *en face*, even though the corresponding crest should really be shown from the side; a peer's as well as a gentleman's helmet is usually shown in profile, regardless of whether the corresponding crest might best be shown *en face*.

In Scotland gentlemen bear a barrel helm (Figs 36, 38 and 317), barons and the heads of clans, the tournament helmet (a baron in Scotland is not a peer but someone who has certain feudal rights).

The mantling in the arms of Queen Elizabeth and the Prince of Wales is gold on the outside, ermine on the inside (Fig. 225). The other members of the royal family wear gold lined with silver. In Scotland peers and certain high officials have red mantling lined with ermine (Fig. 366), while the wreath is of the livery colours, i.e. the shield's principal metal and colour. Otherwise the mantling is usually of the livery colours. In Ireland the mantling is often red with white lining (see Figs 376, 385 and 386).

In Scotland a motto is considered an essential component of the arms and it is normally set above the crest (Fig. 317). The heads of clans and certain other people can also bear the clan's war cry, the slogan, which is sometimes the same as the motto. When there are two mottoes the second may be set below the shield if the blazon so specifies.

192

In England a motto is not considered an essential part of the arms and there are no rules for its position, though it is generally placed below the shield.

In Great Britain supporters are used as a special mark of distinction only accorded to specific categories of persons or institutions. In England they are reserved for the royal family, secular peers (bishops and archbishops do not have supporters), Knights of the Garter, and Knights Grand Cross of other orders, and also for boroughs, counties and certain institutions (Figs 272, 313, 323, 328 and 336).

In Scotland supporters are more common, but must nevertheless be officially registered. Apart from the English categories already mentioned they can also be awarded to the heads of clans and certain ancient families, feudal barons and their eldest sons, Kinghts of the Thistle, and other persons of special merit at the discretion of Lyon King of Arms (Figs 348 and 366).

Crowns and coronets are in Great Britain generally used only by the royal family and the peerage. They are placed above the shield (see Figs 57, 313, 322, 328 and 366). The coronet usually encloses a crimson cap topped by a gold tassel and edged at the base with ermine which is visible below the coronet (p. 68). The helmet and the crest are placed above the coronet (Figs 57 and 313). In Belgium the coronet is borne in a similar way (Figs 422 and 423), but most other countries either do not use coronets together with helmet and crest or else set the coronet on the helmet (Sweden, Poland, Italy, Spain, France).

In Central Europe both titled and untitled nobility and some-times commoners too use a coronet on the helmet which is not a sign of rank (see pp. 18 and 40), but in Great Britain this is rare. In Scotland a crowned helmet can be granted to the heads of certain families. Feudal barons can bear a chapeau or 'cap of maintenance' (see Fig. 217).

Members of Scottish clans who themselves have no right to a coat of arms can wear the crest of their chief as a badge within a belt bearing the chief's motto (see Fig. 361), as a rule in the form of a metal brooch pinned to a cap. A clansman who himself has a right to arms and a motto (Gaelic: *duine uasail*) can bear this or the motto of the head of his clan, as well as an eagle's feather if he is the head of his house (Fig. 360), and the same goes for the chieftain of a sept except that he wears two feathers (Fig. 359). Three feathers indicate the chief of the clan. In Fig. 358 a peer's coronet is also included because the man in this case is also a lord, which the chief of a clan is not bound to be. This shows Lord Reay's badge, as chief of the Clan Mackay. The three other cap-badges are: Fig. 359, Macneill of Colonsay; Fig. 360, Irving of Balgownie; Fig. 361, Davidson of Tulloch.

The badges representing plants on the same page belong to the following clans: Fig. 353, Kennedy, Macduff and Stewart; Fig. 354, Drummond, Macmillan and MacInnes; Fig. 355, Macleod, Macnicol and Ross; Fig. 356, Hay; Fig. 357, Gordon. The thistle, Fig. 352, is Scotland's national flower.

Another special feature of British heraldry is the system of distinguishing various members of the same family with the aid of individual marks of difference introduced into the basic coat (p. 72). The idea behind it is that a coat of arms should identify its bearer, so that a father and son, or two brothers, do not have exactly the same arms. Similar 'cadency marks' have been used on the Continent usually, but not always, among princes and the high aristocracy, but they have never been popular and in most countries went out of use long ago.

This is to some extent the case in England too (apart from the royal family), although the practice has been more prevalent and has remained in use longer than in the rest of Europe. The principle is (or was) that only the head of the family bore the arms without a difference. When the father died, the eldest son took over these original arms by removing the symbol for an eldest son, as a rule the label (Fig. 370). Younger sons on the other hand retained their cadency marks and sometimes these were passed on, with or without further differences, to their descendants. In the course of two or three generations however the system soon becomes so involved and overloaded that it becomes unworkable.

In Scotland the situation is somewhat different because each person who has a coat of arms must have it registered, even though it may have been inherited, and on registration Lord Lyon King of Arms stipulates a difference in conformity with an official system (see Fig. 371). But the truth is probably that comparatively few people take the trouble to register their arms, and it would be too involved to compel them to do so (although in theory Lord Lyon could do so legally).

Cadency marks can be depicted in any tincture though the 'colour rules' (p. 23) should be adhered to. Silver (argent) labels are now generally considered to be the privilege of the royal family; the Prince of Wales has his undecorated, while other members of the royal house vary theirs with roses, crosses, anchors etc.

In addition to the official bodies Great Britain has a large and active heraldic association – The Heraldry Society, 28 Museum Street, London W.C.1.

194

The Netherlands and Belgium (pp. 76-81)

Those areas which today make up the Kingdom of the Netherlands (Holland) and Belgium have had a far more complicated history than the British Isles. At various periods in time these countries have, either wholly or in part, belonged to the Holy Roman Empire, Burgundy, Austria, Spain and France. In 1581 the seven northern provinces declared themselves an independent republic. In 1815 the republic united with the southern Netherlands to form the United Netherlands under William I of Orange-Nassau but fifteen years later, in 1830, the South broke away and became the independent kingdom of Belgium under Leopold of Saxe-Coburg. Thus it cannot be expected that heraldry should have developed in these two countries along such methodical and controlled lines as in Great Britain.

The Netherlands (pp. 76-9)

The armorial bearings of the nobility, in all about 400 at the present time, are in the Netherlands protected by law (against plagiarism and misuse). They are registered by the Council for Patents of Nobility, *Hoge Raad van Adel,* which also keeps a register of civic arms and suchlike. The arms of commoners are not registered and are not protected by law. All the same there is hardly any other country, perhaps with the exception of Switzerland, where the use of coats of arms by bourgeois families is so widespread. The majority of such arms originate from the republican period (1581–1815); according to Netherlands law everybody had a right to assume arms, and there were a tremendous number of families who did so.

There is a great interest in heraldry, and its study is well organised, the centre for it being the Koninklijk Nederlandsch Genootschap voor Geslacht- en Wapenkunde, Bleijenburg 5, The Hague.

There are no specific rules, as there are in Great Britain, about which rank may bear which helmets and in which position. In the Netherlands any coat of arms, whether it belongs to a commoner or to a nobleman, can be used with barrel helm, tournament helmet, barred or visored helmet, in profile or affronty; and if anyone wishes to use more than one helmet there is nothing to stop him.

Something of the same holds good for supporters. They were no doubt originally a privilege of the aristocracy, but that has long been forgotten, and some bourgeois families have supporters, while many noble families do not.

Mottoes are not common, except in the arms of noble families, when they are as a rule in French or Latin. But here again everybody has a right to do as he pleases.

Coronets of nobility (p. 76) are placed above the shield, and formerly helmet and crest were set above this, or the coronet was set on the helmet. Nowadays this is not generally considered good heraldry. Today the general practice is to use either a coronet alone or a helmet and crest. A crowned helmet, purely ornamental and not indicative of rank (pp. 36 and 40) is quite another thing and is used by both aristocracy and commoners (see also Fig. 412).

There is only one type of royal crown, and princes and princesses use the same crown as Queen Juliana (Figs 387 and 412). The arms of Prince Claus, the consort of Princess Beatrix, quarter the lion of the royal house (Nassau) with his father's coat, a castle (von Amsberg). In the crests however the lion stands for Amsberg and the wings for Nassau, both rising out of ordinary crowned helmets.

The title of *burggraaf* (Fig. 391) is no longer borne by any living Dutchman: the coronet is therefore used today only in Belgium. Something of the same is true of the coronets of princes, other than royal, and of dukes (Figs 410 and 411); they date from the years 1815–30, when the Netherlands and Belgium were united, and today are used only in Belgium.

But these coronets are at times used in civic arms. It is a general practice in the Netherlands to include a coronet in the arms of boroughs and the like. Some important cities such as Amsterdam and Nijmegen have variations of the Imperial Austrian crown (see Figs 398 and 567), and certain provinces, e.g. Gelderland, Drenthe and North Brabant, a princely crown (Fig. 406). Lesser towns use the coronets of marquises or counts – nowadays mostly the latter (Figs 394–7). Supporters are much in use (Figs 398 and 406), and the imperial eagle occurs frequently (Fig. 404). Other charges which are common and characteristic of Netherlands heraldry in general are a little bird without beak or feet (a sort of martlet, see Figs 119, 407 and 408) and small 'couped' St Andrew's crosses (Figs 398, 399 and 400). This latter is regarded in the Netherlands as a symbol of justice.

Belgium (pp. 80–1)

Belgium's stormy history is reflected among other things in the heraldry of the Belgian aristocracy. Besides the ancient nobility in the old principalities of Brabant, Flanders, Hainault, Limburg etc., which make up the country, there are families who were ennobled by the Holy Roman Emperors, or by the Spanish, French and Netherlands

196

kings (the latter during the period 1815–30), by Napoleon and since 1831 by the kings of the Belgians. It is hardly to be wondered at that Belgian heraldry is of such a varied nature. Nevertheless there has developed, at any rate since 1831, a specifically Belgian heraldic style.

The helmets are mostly silver or steel-coloured, barred and edged with gold and there is a gold medallion on a gold collar around the neck (Figs 420, 422 and 423). The inside is as a rule red, but blue is also found. Nobility without title use neither coronet nor crowned helmet. Nobility of title (the lowest rank of which is knight – French: *chevalier*, Flemish: *ridder*) can use both coronet and crowned helmet. The coronet is set above the shield, the helmet with its crown and crest above this (see Figs 273, 422 and 423). The shield is often shown hanging by a strap from the helmet (Figs 420 and 422).

For barons and higher ranks supporters are *de rigueur*. In contrast to the usual practice in British heraldry they stand not on a natural base but on an ornamental one (see Figs 273 and 415). Most of such coats of arms also include a motto.

The royal family have a gold visored helmet with raised visor, red on the inside and surmounted by the royal crown. The king and queen have their helmets set affronty, while the Duke of Brabant (the heir apparent) and other princes have theirs set in profile. The king's arms – on a field sable a lion rampant or langued and armed gules (see Fig. 415) – are borne without difference by the Duke of Brabant. Other princes bear the arms with a bordure or (Fig. 71b), unless they descend from a Duke of Brabant, in which case they bear a red label with three points (Fig. 370b). Princesses bear the king's arms without difference, but in a lozenge-shaped shield (see Fig. 246) with the royal crown above.

In Belgium's civic heraldry the rampant lion seems to be even more popular than elsewhere and coronets of the nobility are used rather than mural crowns.

Heraldic questions are dealt with by the Office Généalogique et Héraldique de Belgique, Musées Royaux d'Art et d'Histoire, 10, Parc du Cinquantenaire, B-1040 Brussels.

France (pp. 82–9)

The heraldic lily is in people's minds so readily associated with France that it is simply known as the French lily or fleur-de-lys. Lilies were the device of the French kings (pp. 82 and 85) and as such have made an impression which has never been erased, either by the French Revolution (which abolished them) or by two Napoleonic empires and a number of republican constitutions (which replaced them with other devices). And the fact that such lilies are common to the heraldry of nearly every country, not just to that of France, has had no influence on the popular conception that such lilies are 'French'.

The lily was used as a symbol by the French royal house even in pre-heraldic times. At the beginning of the twelfth century it appeared on the coronation robes, the crown and the sceptre. From the end of the twelfth century it was shown on the royal standard, but it is only from the beginning of the thirteenth that proper royal arms bearing the fleur-de-lys are known (on a seal).

Originally an unspecified number of fleurs-de-lys were strewn over the field, as can be seen in derivatives of the arms (see Figs 429 and 447), but from the close of the fourteenth century three was the accepted number (Fig. 424).

In civic heraldry the fleur-de-lys still lives on throughout the whole of France, especially as an augmentation (see p. 54) as a chief in the armorial bearings of certain towns of some importance (see Figs 454–7). As already mentioned the arms of Paris contain a chief with the fleurs-de-lys in their ancient form, and they are similarly included in the arms of all departments of the central province of France, the Ile de France, which, however, is of a more recent date.

In the Middle Ages the French royal house differenced its arms for the various princes or lines (see also p. 181). The heir apparent, *le dauphin* (=dolphin), had the royal arms quartered with a blue dolphin on a gold field (see Fig. 444), and there is a story behind this unusual title. A noble family in the South of France, the Dauphins de Viennois, owned among other estates the province that had been called 'le Dauphiné' after them. In 1349 the last male of the line bequeathed this to the king on condition that the French king's eldest son should bear the family's arms and name to all eternity. The figure of a dolphin was later included in the crown of the French heir apparent (Fig. 426).

Another way of differencing was with the aid of marks of cadency. Charles of Anjou, a younger brother of Louis IX (Saint Louis), bore a red label. When he conquered Southern Italy and established a kingdom there a chief with fleurs-de-lys and the Anjou label became the badge of his followers (see Fig. 718). Subsequent Dukes of Anjou used the difference of a red bordure (Fig. 447) and several hundred years later the label was used once more by the French prince who in 1700 became King of Spain as Philip V.

A white label was borne in the fifteenth century by the Dukes of Orléans (Fig. 448) and this difference has since remained a constituent of the arms on the Orléans side of the French royal house. Another famous mark of difference in the French royal arms is the red bend of the Dukes of Bourbon (Fig. 446).

Differencing was originally used by people other than members of the royal family, but it gradually fell into disuse.

In France coats of arms are protected by law, and it is punishable to use the arms of others. On the other hand everybody is free to assume armorial bearings, provided they are not already in existence. The Association de la Noblesse Française was established in 1932 and to be a member you have to prove that you belong to the aristocracy. There is no institution for the registration and supervision of coats of arms.

In former times there was, however, for in 1407 King Charles VI instituted a college for the French heralds, at the head of which was a specially appointed heraldic official. In 1616 the office of Juge Général d'Armes de France (Judge General for French Arms) was established and the holder had two main tasks. He had to deal with disputes between people who could not agree on who had the right to a certain coat of arms, and he had to ensure that new coats were designed in conformity with the rules of good heraldry. The conferment of new arms and the confirmation of existing arms were also his responsibility. From 1641 up to the French Revolution in 1789, when all traditional heraldry was abolished and prohibited, it was always the same family, that of d'Hozier, who held this office of heraldic judge.

Among burghers, merchants, craftsmen and farmers coats of arms were common as early as the thirteenth century and in 1696 their number was greatly increased. That year King Louis XIV, in order to obtain money for his wars, introduced a tax on escutcheons, and many who did not already possess one immediately had a coat of arms bestowed on them. From the purely heraldic point of view the result was, among other things, a tremendous list, the *Armorial Général*, which still exists. Of its *c.* 110,000 coats of arms, about ninety per cent of which are those of commoners, it is believed that about two-thirds were created for the occasion, to provide money for the Treasury. It should be noted, however, that commoners were forbidden to use a helmet and crest.

Quite contrary to the *Armorial Général* and to the country's traditions, King Louis XV tried in 1760 to enforce that only the aristocracy were entitled to bear arms, but the attempt failed. However, thirty years later the Revolution, as mentioned above, abolished all traditional heraldry, both for commoners and for the nobility. After Napoleon became Emperor in 1804 he introduced his own, imperial heraldry, the most characteristic feature of which was a consistent regimentation and regulation (see pp. 90–3 and 201 ff.). After Napoleon the old heraldry was to some extent revived. When the monarchy was restored and the second empire established, offices were instituted which among other things had to deal with titles of nobility and armorial bearings, but these offices no longer exist. Nowadays there is a great interest in civic heraldry.

Before the Revolution the French kings bore a gold helmet with raised visor, red on the inside and set affronty (Fig. 440). It was as a rule surmounted by the royal crown, was richly decorated and had the collar of the Order of the Holy Spirit around the neck. Nobles had silver or steel-coloured barred helmets with edges and grills of gold. Dukes and marquises had the helmet affronty, counts and lesser ranks, in profile (p.88). The number of bars might indicate the rank, from eleven for a duke to three for a noble without title, but the system varied and was not always adhered to. The visored helmet in profile was the rule for new aristocracy without a title (Figs 458 and 461), but it could also in certain cases be used affronty by dukes.

A coronet was set above the shield surmounted by a helmet (Figs 459 and 460), but later it became the custom to set the coronet on the helmet or omit the helmet altogether (Figs 462 and 463). Members of the nobility without title have no coronet.

Pair de France was originally an office, and later became an honorific title which could be bestowed on a noble regardless of his rank. A *pair de France* was entitled to a robe of estate (Figs 459 and 464). Under the restored monarchy at the beginning of the nineteenth century the robe was blue, bordered and decorated with gold and lined with ermine, and surmounted by a coronet (Fig. 434).

Supporters are common in the armorial bearings of the French aristocracy, but unusual for commoners; there are however no hard and fast rules for their use. If there is a motto, and it stems from a war-cry, it is as a rule set above the achievement.

Heraldic association: Société Française d'Héraldique et de Sigillographie, 113 Rue de Courcelles, Paris 17.

Napoleonic Heraldry (pp. 90–3)

When Napoleon became emperor in 1804 he did not assume the arms of the Buonaparte family (Fig. 469) as his imperial escutcheon, but adopted a completely new one: an eagle with a thunderbolt in its claws, clearly inspired by the eagles of the ancient Roman legions (see Fig. 11).

For his new, imperial aristocracy Napoleon devised a heraldic system which was to some extent based on the old heraldry from before 1789, but which at the same time contained many new details and was different because of the standardisation, or even compartmentalisation, it symbolised. The idea behind the system was that it should reflect the Napoleonic state, especially the army, and this new heraldry became so regimented in its categories that the individual characteristics of the various coats of arms almost disappeared. The stereotyped patterns given as examples on pp. 91–3 show the empty shields which were all that was left for the personal arms of the holder. It was the same with civic heraldry (Figs 487–9). Furthermore, even in those cases where there was a free choice the designs became very repetitive, because so many people chose the same bearings: sabres, swords, cannon, grenades, pyramids, bridges and suchlike, inspired by the campaigns of those days. The royal fleurs-de-lys disappeared completely and were replaced by bees (Figs 467, 472 and 487).

Helmets and crests as well as supporters and mottoes were excluded. The coronet was replaced by a black velvet cap or 'toque' (French: *barrette*) (pp. 91 and 92). The fur at the edge, the clasp at the front and the number of white ostrich feathers indicated the rank. Both a non-royal prince and a duke had a gold clasp and seven plumes, but the prince had an edging of miniver (or 'vair'), in contrast to the ermine edging of the duke (Figs 473 and 474). A count had an edging of ermines (white spots on a black field, see Fig. 62), with a clasp half of which was gold and the other silver, and five plumes (Figs 277 and 475). A baron had an edging of counter-vair, a silver clasp and three plumes (Fig. 476). The cap of a knight (*chevalier*) had green edging and a single tuft of white horse hair (Figs 485 and 486).

The highest ranks had mantles or robes of estate. A non-royal prince's mantle was blue strewn with gold bees and surmounted by another cap with ermine edging (Fig. 472). A duke's mantle was blue with a lining of vair, while the mantle for a count who was also a senator was blue with a white lining.

Embellishments reminiscent of mantling or lambrequins issued from the cap of rank (p. 92). Princes and dukes had six of these, all gold. Counts had four, two gold, two silver. Barons had two silver, and knights had none.

With the aid of specified content and tincture classification could be carried even further. All non-ruling princes had a blue chief strewn with yellow bees (Fig. 472), and all dukes had a red chief strewn with white stars. All counts had a blue dexter canton with an emblem which further indicated their position in life e.g. senator, officer or archbishop (Figs 478, 479 and 480). All barons had a similar, but red, sinister canton (Figs 481 and 482). Knights of the Legion of Honour bore the cross of the Order on a red ordinary, usually a pale or a fess (Figs 285 and 485). See also Italy, p. 213.

Women bore oval shields between two palm branches, gold with a blue knot for a countess, silver with a purple bow for a baroness. Both categories had also an oval inescutcheon, yellow for a countess, white for a baroness.

In civic heraldry there were three grades of 'important towns', and the attributes of their rank can be seen in Figs 487–9.

With the return of the monarchy this heraldry disappeared from the official scene until it was revived under Napoleon III (1852–70).

Germany and Austria (pp. 94–111)

In the year 962 the German King Otto the Great was crowned emperor by the Pope, and this marked the beginning of the imperium which was later given the name of the Holy Roman Empire of German Nation. It lasted until 1806, when Emperor Franz II abdicated. In 1804 however he had also assumed the title of Emperor of Austria, and during the years 1804–6 he was thus both German and Austrian emperor. The Austrian empire continued until 1918 but it was superseded by Prussia in political power, and in 1871 the King of Prussia was elected German emperor as William I.

These events were of great importance even beyond the frontiers of Germany and Austria, because the Holy Roman Empire and the Austrian empire comprised far more countries than these two. Wholly or in part, permanently or periodically, the Netherlands, Switzerland, Savoy, Northern Italy, large areas of the Balkans, Hungary, Bohemia and large parts of Poland belonged to one or the other of these German-speaking empires, and this has left its mark on the heraldry of these countries.

All three empires mentioned took the eagle as their heraldic ensign. In ancient Rome the eagle symbolised Jupiter, and it was no doubt on the Roman pattern that the emperors took the eagle as their device (see Figs 11 and 12). An eagle with two heads was known from the Byzantine Empire, and from the beginning of the fifteenth century the custom was established that the ordinary eagle should be the device of the German king before he was crowned emperor, while the double-headed eagle would be the ensign of the crowned emperor (see p. 7). But there were many exceptions to this rule.

Free cities, also called imperial cities, i.e. cities owing allegiance only to the emperor, emphasised this by having the imperial eagle charged with an inescutcheon of their own coat of arms, or by bearing the eagle by itself (Fig. 538). Other combinations also occur – see Fig. 606.

In hundreds of Italian coats of arms there is an 'imperial chief', or *capo dell' impero*, as a declaration of political allegiance (Fig. 718), and as a sign of favour certain princes of the Holy Roman Empire were given the right by the emperor to superimpose their own arms on the imperial eagle (Figs 792 and 884).

When the Austrian empire was established in 1804, the double-headed eagle was continued (Fig. 567), but when the new German empire was founded in 1871, an eagle with only one head was chosen as its emblem, probably to emphasise the distinction. It appeared black on a yellow field. On its breast it bore a shield with the arms of Prussia, also an eagle, but black on a white field (Fig. 492; the red bordure of this coat is a difference for the crown prince).

When the Weimar republic was set up in 1918, the old German eagle was retained as an emblem, although in a modernised form, and this was adopted by West Germany, the *Bundesrepublik Deutschland,* after the Second World War (Fig. 494). The colours black, red and yellow in the coat of arms are the same as those of the present German flag and they originate from the German wars of liberation against Napoleon at the beginning of the nineteenth century.

In 1919 the Republic of Austria took as its arms an eagle with only one head as the background for a red shield with a white fess (Fig. 570). This shield stems from the arms of the family of Babenberg which ruled in Austria up to 1246; after that time its coat of arms gradually developed into the arms of Austria. Instead of the sceptre, sword and orb (see Fig. 567) the republican eagle holds a sickle and a hammer and is ensigned with a mural crown, these three things symbolising the farmers, the industrial workers and the bourgeoisie. After the liberation from Nazi Germany in 1945 the broken fetters around the eagle's claws were added.

In the Holy Roman Empire, as elsewhere, the oldest coats of arms were self-assumed, but from the close of the fourteenth century emperors began to grant arms, as time went on mostly through specially appointed officials called *Hofpfalzgrafen* or *Pfalzgrafen*, (literally translated 'palace counts') (in this connection the word has nothing to do with the principality of Pfalz (the Palatinate) on the Rhine). Certain very noble families, including the Tyrolean branch of the Archdukes of Austria, were hereditary 'palace counts', but there were also many others. In time the king only granted arms personally to cities and the like. Family coats were dealt with through the 'palace counts', whether for commoners (the great majority) or for nobles. When raised to the nobility the recipient had the arms which he may have possessed already augmented by the addition of new charges or quarterings. The name for this was *Wappenbesserung*, but according to modern taste the result was nearly always a coat of arms that was heraldically less satisfactory.

In 1702 Prussia established a government office on French lines which also had to deal with the heraldry of the country, especially civic arms, and in 1855 this office became the *Königlich Preussisches Heroldsamt*, which also dealt with ennoblement etc. After the First World War this office was done away with and its archives transferred to the Prussian Ministry of Justice; this is now in Merseburg in East Germany.

Bavaria in 1818 created the office of *Reichsherold*. In 1902 Saxony instituted the *Kommissariat für Adelsangelegenheiten*, and from 1912 until 1918 patents of arms were also granted to the middle classes. Such documents of this commissariat that have survived the Second World War are to be found among the State archives in Dresden. In Württemberg the Ministry for Foreign Affairs assumed responsibility for questions concerning nobility and heraldry.

In Austria this was done by the Ministry of the Interior. Its documents, the so-called *Gratialregistratur*, are kept today among the Austrian State archives in Vienna.

After the First World War the aristocracy in both Germany and Austria was abolished. Nevertheless it is permissible in Germany to use noble titles and styles such as *von*, as these were generally made part of the family name by the Republic of Weimar, though in Austria it is a punishable offence to use any form of noble title.

Nowadays it is characteristic of both Germany and Austria that simple coats of arms are preferred to more complicated ones. Many families of ancient lineage have gone back to using their original plain arms, often designed in mediaeval style (Figs 525–7), instead of the composite arms with their many quarterings and helmets, supporters etc. which their ancestral arms had gradually accumulated. But whether it is a good thing to have a coat of arms made up in a style previous to that of the patent of nobility is quite another question, particularly if it contains a charge, such as a cannon, which belongs to a subsequent period.

The standard form of a German coat of arms proper to the nobility is nowadays as is shown on p. 102: shield and barred helmet with or without coronet, possibly with a medallion around the neck, and with a crest and mantling.

Many of the aristocratic arms depicted in this book have a coronet set above the shield with a helmet or helmets above it (Figs 521, 530, 531 and 580). This was how coats were designed in earlier times, e.g. in letters patent for armorial bearings, but nowadays there is an inclination to get away from such combinations and either a coronet on its own or a helmet with its appurtenances only is preferred. Supporters and mottoes are borne mostly by the higher nobility, but not all of them use them. The custom of having two or more helmets goes back to the fifteenth century. Noble families, with their armorial bearings composed of many quarterings, wanted to have, if possible, an equivalent number of helmets (see Figs 55 and 575).

The earliest arms of non-aristocratic families are known in Germany from the thirteenth century. Throughout the centuries new families have assumed coats of arms, and still do, without interference from any authority. Added to these are the thousands of armorial bearings of commoners which since about 1400 have been granted by the *Pfalzgrafen*. Many of these escutcheons contain ciphers (see p. 104), but these are rarely included in noble arms. Mottoes are not customary. The standard form of a German coat of arms for a commoner is nowadays shield and tournament helmet, with or without wreath, with crest and mantling (see Figs 550, 552, 557 and 562); the barred helmet with crest coronet is also found.

People in Germany are more concerned about 'family arms', *Familienwappen*, than are people in Western and Southern Europe and the British Isles, and the principle of individual members of a family varying their arms is usually foreign to German heraldic ideas. But differencing does occur in a form unlike that in Great Britain and France. Branches of the same family of high rank can difference their arms by various combinations of quarterings, and among the families of commoners we find differences made by a change in crests or tinctures (Fig. 552). The German Crown Prince differenced his arms from those of the Emperor with a red bordure.

There is at the present day a great interest in civic heraldry. New civic arms are constantly being designed and in this connection various forms of mural crown have come into use (Figs 25, 516, and 522). In earlier times an attempt was made to establish a social scale of mural crowns, including a special one for the seat of a reigning monarch, but this did not catch on. Since the mural crown is a comparatively new phenomenon in heraldry, it should not be used in conjunction with arms which have been designed in an earlier style. Civic heraldry also makes use of more traditional coronets (see Figs 270, 518, 519 and 560).

In West Germany it is usual today for the authority responsible for internal affairs in each federal state to grant and confirm civic arms. Family arms are a completely private matter, although they enjoy a certain amount of legal protection under Paragraph 12 of the Federal Law.

There are various heraldic societies in West Germany, the most important being as follows: Der Herold, 1 Berlin 33 (Dahlem), Archivstrasse 12-14, West Berlin; Zum Kleeblatt, Hannover-Kirchrode, Forbacherstrasse 8; and Wappen-Herold, 1 Berlin 31, Tharandter Strasse 2, West Berlin.

In Austria there is the Adler Society, Haarhof 4 a, Vienna 1.

Switzerland (pp. 112–13)

The Swiss federal republic has developed from the three 'forest cantons' of Schwyz, Uri and Unterwalden. They belonged to the dukedom of Swabia, which again was part of the Holy Roman Empire. During the thirteenth century various noble Swabian families, and especially the Habsburgs, seized more and more power, and to counter this the forest cantons sought to come under the direct rule of the Emperor instead of having one of the local princely or aristocratic dynasties as intermediary. In 1291 the farmers of the three cantons formed an alliance (the Oath on the Rütli) to unite against the noble rulers who wanted to have authority over them.

In the course of the fourteenth century Lucerne, Zürich, Bern, Zug and Glarus joined the Confederation, and when the Duke of Austria in 1386 tried to force his will upon it, his army of knights was defeated at the battle of Sempach. After this victory the Swiss achieved their aims: to come under the jurisdiction of the very loosely organised central government of the Empire, which meant in effect almost complete political freedom.

Fribourg (Freiburg) and Solothurn became in 1481 members of the Confederation, and in 1499 the Swiss compelled the Emperor to grant them what amounted to full independence.

At the beginning of the sixteenth century the Confederation was enlarged by the addition of Basel, Schaffhausen and Appenzell, but during the Reformation the country was torn apart by religious struggles. At this time it became more and more common for the young Swiss to enter military service under foreign princes, especially the King of France. The Papal Swiss Guard in the Vatican is a reminder of this particular side of Swiss history.

In 1798 the French revolutionary army marched into Switzerland, annexed Geneva and made the rest of the country into the Helvetian Republic. In 1815, after the fall of Napoleon, the Congress of Vienna laid down that Switzerland should remain neutral for all time.

It is not to be wondered at that Swiss heraldry reflects many different influences. This is true both of the great majority of independently assumed arms and, perhaps to a greater extent, of those coats of arms granted by foreign princes. The oldest in this category date from the beginning of the fifteenth century and were granted by the German emperors and the Duke of Savoy. Subsequent patents were issued by the palace counts (see p. 203), the Duke of Milan, the King of France, the King of Prussia (in his capacity as Prince of Neuchâtel in Switzerland), the Duke of Lorraine, Napoleon, and even the kings of Hungary, Bohemia and England.

Cantonal and civic heraldry is characteristic in its simplicity. Many coats of arms contain no charge at all, the field being divided into two fields by a simple line (Figs 591, 592, 595, 603 and 604). Others are allusive, e.g. the bear of Bern (German: *Bär*), Uri's aurochs (Latin: *urus*) and Schaffhausen's sheep (German: *Schaf*) (see Figs 596, 597 and 605). The arms of Geneva (Fig. 600) are composed of the eagle of the German Empire (the Bishop of Geneva became a vassal of the emperor in 1162) and the key of St Peter (the city's cathedral is dedicated to this saint). Other Swiss cities that wished to emphasise the fact that they owed allegiance to nobody else but the emperor could do as Lausanne did (Fig. 606).

The two family arms at the top of p. 113 are both allusive. A bucket like that in the arms of the Kübele family is called a *Kübel* and the wavy bend in the arms of Gonzenbach illustrates a stream or *Bach*.

Fraternity and guild arms are known from the fourteenth century, first in the form of banners, later as proper escutcheons. Supporters were very common.

As a contrast to the helmets of the age of chivalry and the coronets of the nobility it was customary during the life of the Helvetian Republic (1789–1803) to place Wilhelm Tell's cap of liberty on the shield, and a *Tellenhut* of this type can still be found.

The national arms of Switzerland, the couped white cross on a red field, were already in use as a military banner in Bern in the thirteenth century. They may originate from the time when Bern belonged to Savoy, the arms of this country being a white cross on a red field (see Fig. 206).

Switzerland is perhaps the country where heraldry reaches the peak of its importance. Practically every parish and every farming or bourgeois family has its own coat of arms and uses it, the ancient traditions of democracy no doubt being the basis for this.

Interest in the study of heraldry is considerable in Switzerland and there are several societies. The most important is the Schweizerische Heraldische Gesellschaft, c/o The President: Léon Jequier, 5 Rue Robert-de-Traz, 1200 Genève.

Hungary (pp. 114–117)

In the ninth century tribes of horsemen came from southern Russia and conquered the area which is today called Hungary. Their leader was named Arpad and he founded a dynasty which ruled until 1301.

King Stephen (sovereign prince from 997 and king from 1000 to 1038) broke the power of the ancient tribal chieftains and developed a social organisation of the state which by and large corresponded to that of Western Europe. Stephen later became the national saint of Hungary.

Even before these first Hungarians invaded the country they are supposed to have had various tribal totems or insignia of chiefdom, traces of which are discovered in the eleventh century, and these may be the origin of some of the charges which are most common in the arms of the old Hungarian aristocracy: griffin and bear, as well as sun, moon and stars (Figs 618 and 621).

The first coat of arms in the traditionally Western European form dates from 1190, the first armorial bearings with helmet and crest from about 1300. The first letters patent seem to date from 1326, and the first letters patent in connection with ennoblement from 1430.

A charge which is found very often in Hungarian heraldry is the head of a decapitated Turk, sometimes with turban, sometimes without, but always with a big black moustache and as a rule with blood dripping from the neck (Figs 615 and 617). On occasions the head is held by a warrior, a lion or a griffin, or set on the point of a lance or a sabre. There are heads of Turks in more than fifteen per cent of all Hungarian coats of arms, and the background to this is of course the struggle between Hungary and the invading Turks, which was almost a permanent feature in Hungary's history from the fifteenth century to the eighteenth. Other typical charges are horsemen, rearing horses and an arm with sword in hand (see Figs 618 and 621), also a green dragon which usually has a red cross on its body and which also appears encircling the shield (Fig. 619). This originates from the badge of the Order of the Dragon established by King Sigismund (1387–1437).

The arms of the nobility include both tournament helmet (Fig. 619) and barred helmet, surmounted as a rule by a coronet (Figs 618 and 621). The mantling often has more than two tinctures, and in that case a frequent combination is blue and yellow dexter, red and white sinister (Figs 615 and 618).

The oldest civic arms, assumed by the towns themselves or granted them before the Turkish wars, are influenced by German heraldry and show the usual castles, towers or city walls (Figs 614, 616 and 624). Later civic arms are of a more national character containing charges similar to those in the heraldry of the Hungarian nobility, such as a warrior with sabre or banner, an arm with sword in hand or a beast holding a sword or other items. Shields without charges 'but merely divided into two or more fields are very rare. One example is Hungary's own original coat of arms, which is horizontally striped in red and white (see Fig. 609).

Portugal (pp. 118–19)

Heraldry came to Portugal in the second half of the twelfth century. In the course of the following centuries heraldic authorities may also have been established, for about 1400 King John I (1385–1433) issued detailed instructions to the heralds as to their duties and the territories in which they were to exert their authority. He was probably prompted in this by his father-in-law, the English prince John of Gaunt. His decisions however met with strong opposition among the nobility of the country, among the lesser nobility especially, who were incensed that the king should thus interfere in the way their coats of arms were designed.

The arguments about this continued and at the beginning of the sixteenth century Manuel I (1495–1521) laid down rules for Portuguese heraldry. Commoners were forbidden to bear arms, and an official register was established, the *Livro do Armeiro Mor*, of all approved bearings. New arms were only rarely granted, the reason perhaps being that it is quite usual in Portugal to bear the arms of female ancestors if one so wishes (see below). In this manner far more people can inherit a coat of arms than if they were only hereditary through the male line, and thus the number of people without arms was far fewer.

In its final form heraldic administration in Portugal was organised as follows: there were three Kings of Arms, three heralds and three pursuivants (see p. 180). Two of the officials in each group were in charge of their own part of the home country, while the three remaining had authority in Portugal's territories in India, Goa and Cochin. This is possibly the only known example of European heralds having a sphere of activity exclusively outside Europe (apart from England's Carolina Herald appointed in 1705).

The quarrel between the royal heralds and the aristocracy continued right up to 1910, when both the monarchy and all aristocratic privileges were abolished. Since then anybody who wishes to assume armorial bearings has been able do so. In 1930 however the republican government instituted an office, the *Gabinete de Heraldica Corporativa*, which was responsible for the arms of corporations and professional organisations. These are of great importance in Portugal, where numerous public and private bodies have armorial bearings. Municipal heraldry is supervised by the heraldic commission of the Associação dos Arqueólogos Portugueses.

One of the rules that were laid down was that no civic coat of arms should consist of more than one field: the charge or charges should be set on an undivided shield. The royal coat of arms or the republican edition of it (Fig. 626) must not be included in a civic coat of arms, with the exception of the centre five blue shields with their five roundels (called *quinas* in Portuguese heraldry) which could be retained if justified on historical grounds (see Fig. 635). There were also rules for the use of mural crowns (p. 119): Lisbon and the provincial capitals bear the crown in gold with five towers, other towns a silver crown with four or five towers.

In Portugal people are of the sensible opinion that a person is descended as much from his female ancestors as through the male line. Hence a person can choose to bear his mother's surname, or that of any other ancestor for that matter, as well as his father's. Quite often a son does not use the same surname as his father and frequently two or more brothers have different names.

Heraldry is considered in the same light. The eldest son usually bears the coat of arms of the male line, either by itself or combined with other escutcheons. Younger sons, on the other hand, can choose from among all the arms of their ancestors, using one or more, but no more than four, different coats at a time. They are however expected to indicate by a mark of cadency which ancestor's arms they are bearing or, if they combine a number of bearings on one shield, which is the one in the first field. A certain mark indicates that it is that of the paternal grandfather, another, the paternal grandmother, a third, the maternal grandfather, a fourth, the maternal grandmother, etc. Sometimes these marks of cadency – lily, half-moon, ring, canton, demi-canton etc. (a label was only used by the royal family) – are also accompanied by a letter of the alphabet, as a rule the initial letter of the ancestor's name in question. The system goes back to King Manuel I's directive in the sixteenth century.

In the nineteenth century it was customary for some of the nobility to use a robe of estate, black lined with ermine.

The Instituto Português de Heraldica, Largo do Carmo, Lisboa 2, is a private organisation which aims at bringing together people interested in heraldry.

Spain (pp. 120–3)

Spanish heraldry contains various special features which often facilitate the distinguishing of Spanish arms from those of other countries. One of the most striking characteristics is the bordure, which is very common, containing at various times castles, St Andrew's crosses, lilies or a chain (see Figs 643, 659, 660 and 661). Some of these bordered coats of arms originate from the time when the arms of a married couple were combined by placing the husband's escutcheon in the centre of the shield, with a miniature edition of his wife's ancestral arms, or a charge from these, being arranged six or more times in a bordure around it. An example of this can be seen in the royal arms of Portugal (Fig. 626); the white shield in the centre is the original Portuguese coat of arms; the red bordure with the castles comes from a marriage with a Castilian princess and is derived from her paternal ancestral arms (see Fig. 639). Sometimes a motto is included in the bordure and thus in fact on the shield itself (Fig. 655), a thing that in other countries would be regarded as poor heraldic practice.

Another characteristic and very common charge is a bend held in the mouths of two dragons or lions, as found in General Franco's armorial bearings (Fig. 641).

In heraldic art, as mentioned previously, the 'metals' – silver and gold – can when necessary be replaced by white or yellow. But the rule is that in the blazonry of a coat of arms either white and yellow or silver and gold are used and not, for example, white and gold, or silver and yellow, or yellow and gold, in the same arms. It is one of Spanish heraldry's specific features that this rule is not necessarily followed, for not only may white and silver be used in the same coat of arms, but they may be found one on top of the other. Thus in Fig. 655 the bordure is silver while the motto it contains is white.

The helmets of the royal family are gold visored helmets set affronty with the visor raised (Fig. 647).

Dukes and marquises have silver barred helmets with the bars etc.

in gold set affronty. A duke has nine bars, a marquis seven (Figs 648 and 649).

Counts, viscounts and barons have the same type of helmet but set in profile, the first two categories with seven visible bars – the difference in rank is shown by the coronet – the baron with five (Figs 650, 651 and 652).

A *hidalgo*, that is a gentleman of old lineage without a title, may use the same type of helmet as a baron though entirely in silver (Fig. 653) or, and this is probably more common, a mixture of visored and barred helmet in profile with raised visor and three visible gold bars (Figs 660 and 661). At times the mantling is made to appear as if it were fixed to the interior of the helmet instead of issuing from the top of it (see Fig. 49).

Titled aristocrats place their coronet on the top of the helmet when one is used. Crests are rare and therefore the helmet is often omitted. In that case a coronet may rest directly on the shield. Untitled members of the nobility who do not have a coronet usually retain the helmet and then use a few ostrich feathers as a crest, as a rule in the same colour as the mantling (Figs 660 and 661). The arms of a grandee (see p. 123) are mostly set within a red robe of estate lined with ermine (Fig. 280). Since the eighteenth century it has been the custom for grandees to place a red cap inside their coronets (Fig. 663).

Anybody may use supporters. They were common in the sixteenth and seventeenth centuries, but seem on the whole to have been dispensed with nowadays.

It is the custom in Spain to use the surnames of both the father and mother, sometimes even those of the grandparents, according to certain defined rules, and the same applies with coats of arms. The coats one chooses to bear and the manner in which they are marshalled on the shield have to be approved and registered with the heraldic registrar, the *Cronista de Armas* (see below).

It is usual to include the arms of paternal grandfather and maternal grandfather in the first and second fields of a quartered coat of arms, and those of paternal grandmother and maternal grandmother in the third and fourth. In the Middle Ages descent from four armigerous grandparents was the proof required for recognition of a *hidalgo's* nobility. If one of the grandparents has no coat of arms, one of the others can be repeated, or the shield can be divided into three: once vertically and once horizontally. If there are more than four coats, the shield can be divided up into a corresponding number of quarterings, or one or more coats can be included in an inescutcheon.

212

In 1931, when King Alphonso XIII went into exile, Spain became a republic for the second time (the first was 1873–74), and titles of nobility and armorial bearings were abolished at the same time. In 1939 the Spanish Civil War ended in victory for General Franco, and in 1947 he declared that Spain was again a kingdom (although without a king for the time being). In 1951 an office was established under the Ministry of Justice which was to register and supervise the heraldry of the country.

The officials in control of this work are no longer called Kings of Arms and heralds, as they were formerly, but 'heraldic registrars' – *Cronistas de Armas*. There are five of them, probably one for each of the five historical kingdoms which make up Spain: Castile, León, Aragon, Navarre and Granada (see Fig. 639). The registrars hold office for life and deal not only with the country's heraldry but also with questions regarding titles of nobility and so on.

A coat of arms is in Spain protected by law, and misuse is punishable. Only arms registered with a *Cronista de Armas* can be publicly displayed, but anybody, including a commoner, can register his arms or request the authorisation of a newly composed coat of arms. Whether earlier heralds' patents of arms also conferred nobility has been the subject of much discussion, but a 'certificate or arms' from a *Cronista de Armas* certainly does not do so.

People in former Spanish colonies, e.g. the Americas and the Philippines, who are not necessarily of Spanish descent, can also register an existing coat of arms or obtain a certificate for a new one from the registrars in Spain.

The civic arms of Valencia and Barcelona are set on a lozenge-shaped shield following an old tradition (Figs 644 and 646) that probably has no parallel elsewhere. Instead of the coronet of a marquis on Valencia's shield a royal crown is sometimes used. The mural crown (Fig. 642) was used especially during the time of the two republics (1873–74 and 1931–39), but since then has been replaced almost everywhere by other types of crown.

Bohemia (p. 124)
See under 'Germany and Austria', p. 202.

Italy (pp. 125–33)
In order to understand the many different foreign influences that are found in Italian heraldry, it must be remembered that for practically the whole of its history the country has been the background for power struggles by foreign states, and that in fact large parts have been ruled

directly from abroad or by foreign princely houses for very long periods.

From 1194 Southern Italy belonged to the German Hohenstaufens. In 1266 it was conquered by Charles of Anjou, a French prince (see Fig. 718), whose descendants ruled the country during the following centuries. In 1504 Spain took possession of Naples, which became a bridgehead for Spanish power and influence in Italy for almost 300 years. At the close of the eighteenth century the Spanish were superseded by another collateral branch of the French dynasty who gave this Southern Italian kingdom the name 'The Two Sicilies'.

Central Italy consisted mainly of papal possessions with Rome as their centre, and in Northern Italy there developed in the fourteenth and fifteenth centuries a number of rich and powerful city states, of which Genoa, Florence, Venice and Milan were the most important. But in 1494 Northern Italy was turned into a battlefield on which the Habsburgs, Spain and France fought for the wealth of Italy. In 1540 the Spaniards took Milan and this, combined with their occupation of Southern Italy and Sicily, gave them the upper hand in Italy during the sixteenth and seventeenth centuries. In 1713 however the most important of the Spanish possessions in Northern Italy were ceded to Austria, which then became the dominant power until the French revolutionary armies forced their way across the Alps in 1792. In 1796 Napoleon conquered Lombardy and in 1805 he made himself king of Northern and Central Italy. His stepson, Eugène de Beauharnais, became viceroy of Italy and introduced the Napoleonic system of heraldry (see pp. 90–3).

Theoretically Italy was not a part of the French empire but an independent kingdom, and attempts were made to emphasise this by permitting Napoleonic heraldry as used in Italy to diverge somewhat from the French. For example, in France the Napoleonic counts bore a small blue canton containing one charge or another (see Figs 478, 479 and 480). This canton was green in Italy, corresponding to the newly-created Italian flag which was striped vertically green, white and red in contrast to the blue, white and red of the French tricolour.

After the fall of Napoleon Austria once again took control of Northern Italy, but in 1848 Piedmont began its fight for liberty, and with the help of the French, the Austrians were driven out of Lombardy in 1859. This fight for freedom spread throughout the whole of the country, and in 1861 Victor Emanuel II of Piedmont and Sardinia, of the House of Savoy, was hailed as king of a united Italy. In 1946 King Victor

Emanuel III abdicated in favour of his son Umberto II who ruled until 13 June 1946; he left Italy but never renounced his rights.

During the monarchy a heraldic administration was set up which dealt with the whole country, the Heraldic Tribunal or *Consulta Araldica*. This was abolished by the republic, and later the National Heraldic Council for Italian Nobility or *Consiglio Araldico Nazionale del Corpo della Nobiltà Italiana* was instituted on a private basis, its functions including the registration of noble armorial bearings. In 1853 the *Collegio Araldico* was established in association with the Holy See and this also is mostly concerned with the aristocratic side of heraldry.

As well as all the usual forms of shield, a number of shapes are used in Italy which may be seen in other parts of Europe, but which nevertheless are very characteristic of Italy. Among these are the almond-shaped shield (Figs 26, 35 and 690) and the so-called horse-head shield (Figs 868, 874, 879 and 899). The latter is reminiscent of a horse's head seen from the front, and it is very likely that small shields like these were placed on the foreheads of horses at tournaments. Women's shields are often oval.

The illustrations of noble and other armorial bearings on pp. 125–33 show how they should look 'officially'. Consulta Araldica realised however that many foreign influences had gained a foothold over the years, and accepted that a wide variety of choice in heraldry was now an established fact. The various heraldic systems each had its own type of coronet, and in continuation of a practice dating from the eighteenth century it was permitted to bear in the same coat of arms two different coronets to indicate rank, one above the shield and one on the helmet (Fig. 690). In fact it is possible to have two different coronets showing different ranks, e.g. if one belongs to a family whose head bears a higher title than oneself. In that case the personal coronet is borne above the shield and the superior rank of the head of the family is shown by the coronet on the helmet (Fig. 695).

Another peculiarity of Italian heraldry is the use of both wreath and coronet on the helmet. In most other countries one of these is usually considered sufficient (pp. 36 and 39–40). The Italian wreath is however very slim in comparison with that of other countries and is easily overlooked (Fig. 219 and pp. 127 ff.).

Supporters are rare. When they occur it is usually in the arms of the higher aristocracy, but there seem to be no rules for their use, and in fact it is a case of do-as-you-please.

Under the monarchy the Consulta Araldica registered not only coats of arms of the nobility but also those of 'outstanding' bourgeois families who could prove that they had borne arms for at least a century. Besides these there must be a large number of non-aristocratic arms, especially in Northern Italy. The helmet for a commoner's arms is 'iron-coloured' and visored, with the visor lowered, shown in profile (see p. 19). Crests are rare in Italy, and are not used by commoners.

A 'patrician' is comparable with an untitled nobleman. His helmet is steel- or silver-coloured with raised visor in gold, shown in profile (Fig. 714), and often chased and ornamented. There are many different patrician coronets. This book shows three (Figs 687, 693 and 714), and there is also a special Venetian patrician coronet.

The helmets of the nobility are silver with visor and bars in gold. The more bars there are (pp. 127 ff.), the higher seems to be the rank of the bearer, but there appear to be no definite rules. In fact, any sort of helmet may be used by all classes. Fig. 695 shows a typical form, a visored helmet in profile with only the lower part of the visor open. The helmets of the royal family were golden. The clergy and women have no helmet.

Princes and dukes who have a mantle or robe of estate can set their helmets together with appurtenances on top of the mantle (Figs 696 and 886), and this is not done in any other country.

Civic heraldry is remarkable in its simplicity (see p. 130). The cross is very common (p. 133), so common in fact that two different towns sometimes have the same coat of arms. Initials are also used quite often in civic coats, one example being Rome's (Fig. 674), where the letters SPQR stand for *Senatus Populusque Romanus*, 'the Senate and People of Rome'.

Civic bearings are often ensigned by mural crowns (Figs 688 and 689) or by noble coronets in memory of ancient privileges. Messina and Otranto even have a royal crown. Supporters are rarer, but sometimes the shield is encircled by branches of olive or oak.

As well as the Collegio Araldico, 16 Via Santa Maria dell'Anima, Rome, those interested in heraldry can communicate with the Istituto Italiano di Genealogia e Araldica, Palazzo della Scimmia, 18 Via dei Portoghesi, Rome.

Denmark (pp. 134–7)

In Denmark the use of an escutcheon in the traditional sense was probably introduced during the reign of Valdemar the Great (1157–82). It seems more than likely that the king had armorial bearings containing the three lions (Fig. 727) which are still the arms of Denmark, in spite

216

of the fact that the oldest version of them now extant dates from about 1190 and was his son Canute IV's seal. Two manuscripts, one German and one French, dating from about 1280, are the earliest to record the tinctures. The small red charges around the lions are nowadays usually interpreted as hearts – as the Danish song states, lions leap on the shield and hearts are afire – but they actually represent leaves. There were originally many more of them and their number was uncertain, but in 1819 it was set at nine. The crowns worn by the lions were added by Valdemar the Victorious (1202–41), but in every other respect this coat of arms is much the same now as it was 800 years ago.

The arms of the nobility and clergy are preserved on seals dating from the second half of the same century, and those for farmers from around 1300, but all these various classes may well have had arms previous to these examples which have only by chance been preserved. The same is true, of course, of coats of arms for boroughs, districts, guilds and corporations, all of which are known from seals that go back to the thirteenth century.

When speaking of noble and non-noble (commoners') arms, we should remember that in principle there was no difference originally between them. It was not until much later with the use of features such as coronets and the position of the helmet etc. to indicate the holder's rank, that it was possible to distinguish between the arms of a burgher and those of a nobleman. This in the case of Denmark was after the inception of the Absolute Monarchy in 1660. The difference was made with accessories like those mentioned, never with the charges or the crest.

The earliest coats were very simple, and the arms of the family of Brahe are a good example (Fig. 740), but aristocratic bearings which were obviously made up from two others (such as those of the family of Ahlefeldt, Fig. 742) are known from as early as the thirteenth century. During the fourteenth century the royal family and its branches began to include more than one escutcheon in their shields to indicate possessions, descent or marriage, and about 1398 King Eric of Pomerania had five coats of arms marshalled on one escutcheon. These were the arms of his three Scandinavian realms, one for Denmark, one for Norway and two for Sweden (the ancient Swedish lions and what were then the comparatively new three crowns of Sweden), as well as his father's, arms of Pomerania. They were marshalled on a quartered shield with an inescutcheon, and the four quarters of the main shield were separated by a cross which was no doubt inspired by the Danish flag, the *Dannebrog*.

This version of the royal arms was retained by all subsequent Danish kings. Certain quarterings were dispensed with, others were added or took their place, but the way this coat of arms looked up until 1972 (Fig. 723) was in fact a direct continuation of the combined arms of Eric of Pomerania in 1398. The main shield is divided as follows: the first quarter contains the arms of Denmark (see also Fig. 727); the second quarter, Schleswig (see also Fig. 722), originally a 'reduction' of the arms of Valdemar the Victorious for his son Abel when the latter was the Duke of South Jutland (Schleswig); the third quarter, Sweden's three crowns to commemorate the Kalmar Union, together with the ram of the Faroes and the polar bear of Greenland, both dating from the seventeenth century. Up to 1948 Iceland's falcon was also included. The fourth quarter contains two imaginary charges from the thirteenth century to illustrate the king's suzerainty over the Goths and Wends. The four quarters of the inescutcheon show the king's titles as Duke of Holstein, Stormarn, Ditmarschen and Lauenburg. The centre shield contains the family arms of the Oldenburg dynasty, two bars gules on a field or, with Delmenhorst. The primitive men as supporters were introduced by Christian I in the middle of the fifteenth century, and the mantling was added at the time of the Absolute Monarchy. Below the shield are the collars of the Order of the Dannebrog and the Order of the Elephant.†

The marshalling of the royal arms was not the only heraldic innovation of Eric of Pomerania. He seems to have had an interest in heraldry and perhaps his Queen, Philippa, shared this interest. She was an English princess, from a court intensely preoccupied with heraldry, and the granddaughter of John of Gaunt, who had a considerable influence on heraldic reform in Portugal about this time (see p. 209). The earliest known grants of arms in Denmark to individuals date from the time of Eric of Pomerania. In 1437 the city of Malmö was granted arms containing a griffin's head, which was derived from the King's own Pomeranian charge of a griffin, and this head can still be seen on the lamp-posts and buses in Malmö. A number of murals of armorial bearings, including some on show at Kronborg, date from this time.

It was not of course Eric of Pomerania personally who had these

† On the accession of Queen Margrethe in 1972 the royal achievement was somewhat simplified. The arms for the Goths and Wends in the fourth quarter were eliminated and replaced by Denmark, repeated from the first quarter; the two inescutcheons were replaced by a single inescutcheon bearing only the two bars of Oldenburg; and the limbs of the cross were carried to the edges of the shield—Ed.

measures carried out. He had inherited a heraldic organisation with Kings of Arms, heralds and pursuivants which can be traced back to the early years of the fourteenth century. The kings who succeeded him used the heralds not only for heraldry, but also for other tasks, especially diplomatic ones. When the Kalmar Union ended at the beginning of the sixteenth century the office faded out, although the term 'herald' was retained for certain ceremonial court officials for about another 300 years. In 1938 an office known as the Statens Heraldiske Konsulent (National Heraldic Advisor) was instituted, responsible for heraldic issues in the country. Local authorities too have the right, but not the duty, to seek his advice.

In the course of the sixteenth century it became usual for the nobility to marshal four coats of arms on an escutcheon, either the arms of the four grandparents or both parents of a married couple. But these quartered arms were not hereditary. Marshalling several coats of arms into permanent hereditary armorial bearings really got started after the Absolute Monarchy had been introduced in 1660. The outcome was that not only could all existing arms be combined in one escutcheon, but it was also possible when a completely new coat of arms had been assumed or granted to have it divided into several fields. A good example of this is the Tordenskjold coat of arms dating from 1716 (see Fig. 743). The way in which ancient and simple coats of arms were almost eclipsed by the new fashions can be seen by comparing Figs 742 and 728.

The royal crowns and aristocratic coronets (p. 135) were introduced with Christian V's rules governing rank and precedence in the 1670s and 1680s. They were so rigidly defined that different coronets were specified for use outside and inside the shield (e.g. on an inescutcheon), but these stipulations were not adhered to for very long, not even by the royal chancellery which issued the patents of nobility. In 1679 Christian V gave certain officials ('royal functionaries') the privilege of bearing a barred helmet, in profile and with four visible bars, but no Danish king ever attempted to enforce special types of helmets specifically for the aristocracy.

All the same one often comes across the expressions 'noble helmet' and 'noble shield' in this period. But apart from the fact that the barred helmet probably was regarded by many people as the privilege of the nobility (see Figs 728 and 729), these expressions merely meant 'a helmet borne by a person of noble rank' or 'a shield borne by a person of noble rank'. In Denmark, as already stated, there has never been any difference between the arms of titled persons and

219

those without title, apart from the coronet, not even during the Absolute Monarchy.

As well as raising many people to the rank of nobility, Christian V granted a large number of letters patent conferring the right to armorial bearings, which probably did not imply nobility (the question has been under discussion), but the great majority of middle-class arms – for the clergy and men of learning, officials and officers, businessmen, craftsmen, printers and apothecaries and so on – continued to be self-assumed. How many there are is difficult to say. The aristocratic arms are accountable: there are something between 1,700 and 2,000. But there are far more of the others, at least 8–10,000. In comparison with other countries, such as Sweden, Holland and England, this is a relatively small number, and this is no doubt partly a result of the fact that the farmer class had no influence on political life, anyhow from the time of the civil war known as the Feud of the Count, 1534–36, partly a consequence of the near-impotence politically of practically all classes of the community during the Absolute Monarchy (1660–1849). However, the arms of commoners are often more attractive than those of the aristocracy, mainly because they are usually less intricate (Figs 738 and 739).

In the course of the eighteenth century and the first half of the nineteenth interest in heraldry diminished at the same time as heraldic taste deteriorated (by modern standards). In the second half of the nineteenth century scholars began to develop an interest in heraldic matters, and this resulted among other things in tomes of publications on seals preserved from the Middle Ages, the majority of which were heraldic, and this interest became more widespread. Most of the market towns had had a device since the Middle Ages, mostly on a seal. Now it became the fashion to set this device on a shield and choose suitable colours. The result was not always a happy one as far as the best heraldry goes, because the figures on a seal – engraved on a small scale and intended to stand out in relief in only one colour – are difficult to transpose into the forms and colours of heraldry (Figs 720 and 741), but the interest was there and sometimes the results were splendid (Figs 721 and 744). New local authorities have increasingly adopted armorial bearings, some 200 since 1900 (see Figs 745 and 746).

In 1959 the Heraldisk Selskab, embracing the whole of Scandinavia, was established. Today it has nearly 600 members, a good third of whom are Danes. The activities of the society include the publication of the journal *Heraldisk Tidsskrift*. A specimen copy and other information can be obtained free from the secretary of the society: Dr Ole Rostock,

Sigmundsvej 8, 2880 Bagsvaerd, who also accepts applications for membership.

Norway (pp. 138–9)

The royal arms of Norway can be traced back to Haakon IV Haakonson (1217–63). Like so many other European rulers he took a lion as his device, gold on a field gules. In the 1280s King Eric the Priest-Hater gave the lion an axe, the attribute of St Olav, the patron saint of Norway, between its front paws, but no change has since taken place and in its present form as a shield without the addition of other arms or quarterings it is one of the simplest and most beautiful national coats of arms in Europe (Figs 747 and 750; with reference to the axe see also Fig. 749).

Arms were adopted by others apart from the royal family during the thirteenth century. The oldest extant example is on a seal belonging to a knight, Basse Guttomson, and dates from 1286. In the course of the following fifty years the number of persons and families with armorial bearings greatly increased, but in 1349 Norway was afflicted by the plague known as the Black Death. As well as the dire consequences it had for Norwegian economic and cultural life, heraldry stagnated, and few new coats of arms are known from the subsequent period. In 1380 Norway was united by personal union with Denmark (this lasted until 1814), but the seat of government was in Denmark, and many of the coats of arms which are known from Norway in the following century are really Danish. But the Norwegian farmers developed a form of personal heraldry in cipher, often with both shield and helmet and sometimes with regular heraldic charges.

In the sixteenth and seventeenth centuries Norwegian trade increased and many foreigners arrived in Norway. The Dano-Norwegian kings began to accept citizens of merit into the aristocracy, and this increased greatly after the introduction of Absolute Monarchy in 1660 (see the arms of the family of Werenskiold from 1697, Fig. 754, and those of Tordenskjold from 1716, Fig. 743). According to Christian V's rules of precedence it was, between 1693 and 1730, sufficient to reach the highest level of rank to be regarded as an aristocrat. For details of coronets, the special helmet for the 'royal functionaries', and Christian V's letters patent, see the text under 'Denmark', p. 219. The same text deals with the organisation of heralds in the fifteenth and sixteenth centuries, since this was common to both Denmark and Norway; one of the realm's two Kings of Arms held the title 'Norway'.

Most of the Norwegian family coats of arms date from the seventeenth and eighteenth centuries, particularly from the period after 1660, when the introduction of Absolute Monarchy had strengthened the position of the middle classes. Some of the armorial bearings belonged to purely Norwegian families such as the Bulls (Fig. 751), others to immigrant families like the Griegs (Fig. 753), who came from Scotland, and in fact Scotland had a noticeable influence on Norwegian heraldry from its very beginnings.

On the part of the authorities there was never any desire to exercise control over heraldry at all. There was complete freedom to do what one liked, and this was taken advantage of in Norway to an even greater extent than in other countries. Not only were coats of arms self-assumed, but they were also altered, so that inherited arms were completely changed or took on a new form. Even in the Middle Ages it had been usual for a son to have a different coat of arms from his father, and for brothers to possess different armorial bearings. Now it became customary for the principal features of a coat of arms alone to be inherited, while details were removed or added, so that each coat assumed the character of personal bearings. Inheritance of arms through the distaff side was quite common, even if the male line already bore arms, especially when the mother was of a higher social standing.

Another feature, known in other countries as well, but especially frequent in Norway, was for a person, because of a chance similarity of name, to assume the arms of another, unrelated family, particularly if the latter family had died out.

A number of Norwegian civic coats of arms date from mediaeval or later seals. The arms of the city of Oslo provide an example of this (Fig. 752). They show St Hallvard, the patron saint of the city, with the instruments of his martyrdom, the arrows he was killed by and the millstone tied around his neck when afterwards he was thrown into the water. At the base of the shield lies the girl whom he tried to rescue from her persecutors. As in so many other countries Norwegian civic heraldry has boomed tremendously in recent decades. The interest taken by counties and local authorities is considerable, and a number of fine bearings have been composed.

This growing interest in heraldry in Norway has also found expression in the establishment a few years ago of the Norsk Heraldisk Forening (which is affiliated with the Scandinavian Heraldisk Selskab, see under 'Denmark'), with some 100 members. Further information can be obtained from the secretary of the association: Hans A. K. T. Cappelen, Bygdøy Allé 123 B, Oslo 2.

(The above review of heraldry in Norway is based mainly on Hans A. K. T. Cappelen's work *Norske slektsvåpen*, Oslo 1969.)

Sweden (pp. 140–5)

The text of this section was prepared by Hans Schlyter.

The heraldry that developed in Sweden in the Middle Ages had no special characteristics, for it was on the whole much the same as that of Denmark and similarly had its roots in German heraldry. All the same the various royal arms of Sweden are of interest: the earliest, from the thirteenth century, with lion motifs, and among them the so-called 'Folkunga' arms; the bearings with three crowns (see Figs 209 and 755) from about 1360; and finally the arms composed in various ways which belonged to the monarchs of the fifteenth century and the beginning of the sixteenth.

The basis for the last-mentioned was the device which from about 1400 was included in the seal of Eric, King of Denmark-Norway-Sweden, also known as Eric of Pomerania, successor to Queen Margrethe. It is quartered by a cross, all four arms of which are of equal size, and in the four fields and the inescutcheon there are five charges, the second field containing the three crowns and the third the Folkunga lion. The great Swedish noble Karl Knutsson, a member of the Bonde family, who was opposed to the Scandinavian Union, was intermittently King of Sweden from 1448. His arms as king quartered the three crowns and the Folkunga lion, with the arms of the Bonde family as inescutcheon (a boat). For a short time Karl was also King of Norway and his arms when king of both countries are quartered by a cross with all four arms of equal size, the quarters containing the three crowns and the Norwegian lion holding an axe, with the arms of the Bonde family as inescutcheon.

In Gustavus Vasa's first royal seal dating from the first half of the sixteenth century, his shield is quartered by the same sort of cross with the three crowns and the Folkunga lion. The inescutcheon contains the arms of the Vasa family, which are a pun on two words, one meaning 'garb' and the other 'vase' (see Fig. 790). These arms formed yet another basis for what with the years became the 'great' Swedish national coat of arms. The cross forming the quartering seems sometimes to have been interpreted as an ornament rather than as an essential component of the arms and at various times it was omitted altogether.

Apart from the fact that the cross was not always present and that for a short while during the time of Gustavus Vasa's successor Eric XIV

223

(1560–8) there were some heraldic arguments – see below, the 'Dispute of the Three Crowns' – the national coat of arms of Sweden remained unchanged in its fundamental composition throughout the centuries. This in spite of the Swedish expansion in the Baltic, Germany and Denmark in the sixteenth and seventeenth centuries and the fact that Finland from 1581 was officially a separate grand duchy with its own coat of arms (see Fig. 782). It is interesting to compare this conservatism with the many changes in the development and composition of royal arms which has taken place for example in Denmark and Great Britain.

A heraldic episode which was debated on the highest political level both in Scandinavia and in the rest of Europe was the so-called 'Dispute of the Three Crowns'. After Sweden had opted out of the Scandinavian Union at the beginning of the sixteenth century, the Dano-Norwegian kings removed the quartering with the three Swedish crowns from their coats of arms. Around the middle of the century Christian III adopted it once more and the Swedish King Eric XIV retaliated by assuming the Norwegian lion with an axe and the three Danish lions in his coat of arms. The controversy about the right to the three crowns played a very important part in the negotiations between the two realms before the outbreak of the Scandinavian Seven Years War (1563–70). It was not solved until the beginning of the seventeenth century, when it was decided that both the Swedish and the Dano-Norwegian kings should have the right to bear them.

Heraldic development in more recent times has seen a rich growth in the arms of noble families. Eric XIV introduced among the Swedish nobility, until then wholly untitled, two titled ranks, i.e. counts and barons, and gradually a system developed to distinguish these new honours in a proper heraldic manner. For example the shields of counts and barons were as a rule quartered (see Fig. 766), or they bore a certain number of helmets (see Figs 761 and 765).

In the second half of the seventeenth century the Riddarhus was built in Stockholm as the official domicile for the nobility, and here is preserved a splendid collection of reproductions of arms of noble families from successive ages. The collection is divided into two main groups: the escutcheons of the ennobled and 'introduced' families, in all some 2,300, which cover the walls of the great hall of the Riddarhus from floor to ceiling, and the 440 or so original patents of nobility and arms which are in the Riddarhus archives.

A heraldic phenomenon that is peculiar to Sweden (and Finland) are the so-called 'coats of arms of provinces'. The idea originated about the time of Gustavus Vasa's death in 1560, and the arms were used officially for the first time during the ceremonies at his funeral. It was later decided to turn certain provinces into dukedoms and the rest into counties (see Figs 757 and 756). The original purpose of the 'arms of provinces' was partly to make clear the extent of the Vasa realm and also, by the devices on the arms, to proclaim the natural riches of each. But it is also possible that these arms were intended as heraldry for the people, the common people of the different provinces. But whatever the reason may have been, these arms have acquired and maintained a special place in the public mind and are still used in every conceivable way, spontaneously and without hesitation. Officially their most important function was, and still is, to be the device on standards of regiments raised in, and bearing the name of, the provinces. In the present century many of these arms have been included in the coats of Sweden's *län*, the administrative districts.

In the early days of heraldry no doubt it was only the great nobles of the country and their families who used armorial bearings. From them the fashion spread, first to those classes of the community who were to become its aristocrats, and then among the burghers of the towns, where the use of a coat of arms was probably stimulated by the know-ledge of such practices in Germany. In the late Middle Ages Germany exerted a great influence on Sweden, and in Stockholm for example a large part of the population was German.

This middle-class heraldry, much influenced by the German, was not able to establish itself to anything like the extent that the aristocratic did. There are hardly any examples of mediaeval Swedish middle-class arms being handed down from generation to generation like those of the nobility.

In the late Middle Ages we find that burghers used their ciphers as charges, but later proper heraldic devices came into general use.

In the eighteenth century it was decided that armorial bearings should be the privilege of the nobility. A royal decree from 1762 stipulated penalties for a 'non-noble' person, *ofrälseman*, who included a 'noble' shield and helmet with raised visor in his seal. The phrasing of the decree could indeed be interpreted in more than one way, but it no doubt inhibited the development of non-noble heraldry for a long time.

The burghers began in the nineteenth century to take an interest in civic heraldry. The designs on the seals of market towns, which in many cases dated right back to the Middle Ages, were used as city arms, and the shield was often ensigned by an ornate mural crown (Fig. 774), as a civic parallel to the coronets of the aristocracy (Figs 767, 768 and 773).

225

Civic arms soon became general, and were a kind of status symbol in so far as they showed the difference between market towns and other local authorities. In time it became the practice for the government to verify and specify city arms, both the old existing ones and the new which were gradually being adopted.

The Swedish city arms which go back to mediaeval seals are as a rule easily distinguished from the others by their designs. They typically include a building or group of buildings which in a lifelike or stylised manner depict the town's particular feature: a castle, a city wall, a barbican, a church etc. The charges are often designed in groups of three. Good examples are Helsingborg, Jönköping, Kalmar and Lund.

Around the turn of the century the decorative arts found a welcome subject in heraldry, but the interest was as a rule directed towards arms that appealed to a wider public: the national arms, county arms, city arms. It is worth noting that the growing labour movement consciously used heraldic emblems on its banners and other insignia for the various trade unions.

The functional architecture that became the fashion about 1930, although rejecting ornamentation, occasionally used coats of arms to enliven façades that would otherwise have been completely bare.

Heraldic art for most of the last hundred years or so tended to copy Gothic and Renaissance models with disregard for contemporary trends in the other arts, but in the 1950s this changed and we now find a distinct influence from modern art. This is expressed in an emphasis on outline and surface, in the use of clear, strong colours and in a general interest in the quality of composition.

From the seventeenth century until the middle of the twentieth Swedish heraldic authority was invested in a State official known as the Riksheraldiker, but he did not have anything like the powers of the English Kings of Arms or the Scottish Lord Lyon (see p. 191). It was and still is the government that verifies coats of arms. In the 1950s the office of Riksheraldiker was replaced by two new authorities, the Statens Heraldiska Nämnd and a heraldic department of the Royal Archives with a *Statsheraldiker* in charge. The Keeper of the Royal Archives and the Royal Antiquarian are hereditary members of the Heraldiska Nämnd. The other members are appointed by the government, one of them on the recommendation of the Royal Academy of Liberal Arts. This concentration of official authorities has no doubt resulted in heraldry's being considered of much greater importance.

Ennoblement and the verification of arms connected with this ceased in 1902. Since then official interest in the design of new personal coats of arms has been limited to those appointed to the Order of the Seraphim, Sweden's highest order. In the same way as the knights of the Order of the Elephant and the Knights Grand Cross of the Dannebrog have a plaque with their arms hung in the Royal Chapel of Frederiksborg Castle, the Knights of the Seraphim have theirs hung in the Riddarholm's chapel in Stockholm (after their death). If a knight of the Order of the Seraphim does not already have a coat of arms, one will be designed for him (see Figs 776 and 777), but whether such newly-designed armorial bearings for this Order can be regarded as family bearings is doubtful.

In that sphere of Freemasonry that is not hidden from the general public there are special arms which make up an integral part of the Masonic Order's activities.

There has been a new development in church heraldry in recent years. Arms have been designed for the various dioceses which as a rule are the result of heraldic form being given to the old diocesan seals. Occasionally a coat of arms has been created for the bishop concerned, or official arms have been designed for him by combining the arms of the see with his personal or family arms (see Fig. 904). However, this episcopal heraldry has little importance for the church in Sweden.

In the 1930s a new heraldic practice was introduced: rural districts and boroughs could now also assume armorial bearings and have them officially recognised. Since then the arms of such local authorities have formed the great majority of new coats of arms, and this is linked with the fact that the importance of civic arms as evocative symbols for local government and community life in general has been increasingly understood. The introduction of a law protecting such arms from misuse, and the fact that once the local council has assumed them the government will approve them, have both contributed to their prestige.

The old division into boroughs, market towns and rural districts has recently been done away with; today there are only *kommuner*. The amalgamation of these now taking place may create problems in civic heraldry, but should also stimulate simplification and an artistic rebirth, and civic heraldry seems to be flourishing in Sweden.

Of the Scandinavian Heraldiske Selskab (see p. 220) about a third of the 600 members are Swedes. There are also two Swedish societies, one in Scania, c/o Jan Raneke, Vallgatan 3, 234 00 Lomma, one in Gothenburg, Västra Sveriges Heraldiska Sällskap, c/o Leif Påhlsson, Fortroligheten 4, 412 70 Göteburg.

Finland (pp. 146–7)

Finland was until 1809 a part of the Kingdom of Sweden, and heraldry developed on broadly the same lines as in Sweden (see p. 223), as shown by the examples given in the pages of coloured plates for Finland.

The canting or allusive arms for the genuinely Finnish Horn family, which is of ancient lineage (Fig. 786), go right back to the Middle Ages, and the same is true of the city arms of Borgå (Fig. 785). The charge in the latter represents either a steel for striking fire or the letter C, for *Castellum* (Latin for 'castle', Finnish: *borg*). The arms for the Egentliga Finland (Fig. 781) were created in 1557 for Gustavus Vasa's son John as Duke of Finland, and the Savolax arms (Fig. 783) form one of the arms of the provinces instituted at Gustavus Vasa's funeral in 1560 to illustrate the extent of the Vasa realm. In modern times it is also the arms for the Kuopio *län*.

The coat of arms of Finland (Fig. 782) goes back to *c.* 1580 and was no doubt meant as a political demonstration in heraldic terms. Duke John had in 1568 become King John III of Sweden. There was personal enmity between him and Czar Ivan the Terrible in Moscow. In 1581 John III took the title of Grand Duke of Finland, and it was about the same time that the coat of arms was designed whose contents were easily understood by all and sundry: the lion (as in Sweden's original Folkunga arms) defending himself with his straight sword while trampling the Muscovite curved sabre underfoot. The white roses on the shield were presumably only meant as ornamentation, without symbolic importance, but later they were construed as representing Finland's nine provinces.

The two city arms (Figs 784 and 790) go back to the first half of the seventeenth century. Vasa received its arms in 1611; the charge, a *vasa*, is taken from the armorial bearings of the Swedish royal family, from which its name also comes. The Cross of Liberty was bestowed on the city in 1918 to commemorate the fact that during the War of Liberation of 1917–18 it was the first seat of government of the new state. The arms of Helsingfors (Helsinki) (Fig. 784) date from 1639.

In 1809 Russia conquered Finland. The Czar became Grand Duke of Finland and Finland's lion was included among the arms which decorated the Czar's double-headed eagle (see Fig. 808).

During the Swedish period there was no fundamental difference between the Finnish nobility and the Swedish, and the Finnish aristocracy had its seat in the *Riddarhus* in Stockholm. After separating from Sweden the aristocracy domiciled in Finland established c. 1818 its own *riddarhus*, the membership of which was gradually increased by nobles who had become naturalised or raised to the aristocracy by the Czar. Ennoblement continued right up to 1912.

The Russian influence on heraldry was slight. It was most noticeable in civic heraldry where it was later to be more or less eradicated (on purely heraldic and aesthetic grounds).

This reflects the great interest in heraldry, and especially the feeling for good modern heraldry, which has characterised Finland ever since the country won its independence in 1917, and to an even greater extent since the Second World War. The last generation or so has seen a growing interest in heraldry, especially civic, in all the European countries, but in no other country has this been so intense or produced such good results as in Finland. As mentioned above some city arms in Finland go back to the seventeenth century and some parish seals date right back to the sixteenth. A number of civic arms – especially of larger towns and market towns – appeared in the eighteenth and nineteenth centuries, but most civic arms, including those of rural districts, were created in the last twenty years. Two examples of these can be seen in Figs 789 and 791. Nowadays all councils – borough, county and rural district – in Finland have armorial bearings, now totalling 565, probably a situation unique in the whole world.

Other fields of heraldry are being studied and developed, such as military heraldry (standards etc.) and family arms (Figs 787 and 788). There are two heraldic societies: one is purely Finnish, the Suomen Heraldinen Seura, c/o Olof Eriksson, Grävlingsvägen 6 D 57, Hertonäs; the other is a branch of the general Scandinavian Heraldiske Selskab (see p. 220), c/o Bo Tennberg, Loveret 1, Jakobstad.

Poland (pp. 148–51)

Polish heraldry differs considerably from that of other countries, both in its appearance and its system. Most of the divisions and charges common to the rest of European heraldry (bend, bar, pale etc.) are almost unknown in Poland. On the other hand many Polish coats of arms have various rune-like and cipher-like charges which are unknown elsewhere (see p. 150). In many cases such emblems have become a form of heraldry (probably to facilitate description) consisting of horse-shoes, half-moons, crosses, arrows etc., but there is little doubt that such arms are closely connected with original cipher arms. Fig. 796 is a good example; its three tournament lances may well once have been a simple figure of three straight lines, something like an X superimposed on an I. There is no consensus among experts about what lies behind the idea of these figures, but most agree that they go back to some form of cipher.

Another special feature of Polish heraldry are the so-called *pro-*

clamatio arms. By this is understood armorial bearings common to several noble families, each with its own name and as a rule having no family relationship with one another.

Some of these *proclamatio* arms are common to more than a hundred families. The record is probably held by the horse-shoe enclosing a cross which is common to 563 families (see Figs 805 and 804c). These arms held in common, or arms of family groups, like all coats of arms of Polish families of ancient lineage, have their own nomenclature, usually different from the names of the families that bear them. Their designation is at times the word for the device itself, but most of them might well be old rallying or war cries used in the past by a family group, clan or tribe. The Latin word for war cry is *proclamatio*, and it is from this that the group of arms takes its name.

It may be another instance of this organisation into family groups that ennoblement in Poland often took the form of adoption. Instead of a person for example being raised to the nobility by royal patent, he was adopted into a family that was already noble. Fig. 797 shows the arms of a family (Wielopolski (-Gonzaga)-Myszkowski), adopted by the Italian princely family Gonzaga in Mantua, whose arms can be seen in the first and fourth quarters of the principal escutcheon.

This procedure is perhaps connected with the extraordinary standing of Polish nobility. All Polish noblemen were in theory equal, and it was particularly the less well off among them, the *Szlachta*, who tried zealously to prevent the Polish kings from introducing orders of precedence within the aristocracy. The majority of Polish titles – baron, count, marquis, prince – are of foreign origin, especially German, Austrian, Russian and Papal. Native Polish titles, granted by the kings, were extremely rare and seldom hereditary. But Polish kings could on the other hand invest foreigners with Polish titles of nobility.

In the coats of arms in Figs 796, 802 and 805 the coronet is set on the helmet, but just as frequently we find it ensigning an inescutcheon (see Fig. 797), in which case there may also be a coronet on the helmet. Barred helmets were as likely to be used as the tournament helmet shown in the three examples.

There are thought to be at least 5,000 Polish coats of arms. There may be even more burgher and farmers' arms, a few of which date back to the thirteenth century, but the majority come from the sixteenth century and later, and in addition to these there are over 1,000 ancient city and rural arms. Most of the burgher and civic arms have been lost as a result of Poland's unhappy history. By the Partitions of Poland in 1772, 1793 and 1795 the country was in turn swallowed up by Russia,

Austria and Prussia, and one of the expressions of Polish nationality which was subsequently suppressed was its heraldry. Russia was particularly guilty in this respect. When in the nineteenth century the Czarist regime reluctantly gave ten Polish administrative districts permission to have coats of arms, it was on the condition that these armorial bearings should in no way contain or even be reminiscent of the older devices of these localities. The Germans during the Second World War tried to find the ancient Polish civic seals and those discovered were destroyed.

All the same not everything had been destroyed or forgotten. When after the First World War Poland had once again become independent, the use of many old city arms was resumed and new civic arms were created. What the situation is like today is not certain. But Poland, alone of all the Communist countries, still uses its old coat of arms, a white eagle on a red field. These were originally the armorial bearings of the Polish kings and can be traced right back to the thirteenth century. The bordure, which can be seen in Fig. 795 and which is inspired by Polish military uniforms, was only used between the two wars. After the last war the crown, which the eagle had borne since the Middle Ages, was omitted.

Russia (pp. 152–8)

Heraldry developed late in Russia. In the western part of the country the nobility, being influenced by Poland, began to assume armorial bearings during the course of the fifteenth century, but further to the east, not until the following centuries. Devices were used on seals and as ornaments but were never used in Russia as heraldic military symbols or even for tournaments. The result has been that the divisions of the shield and other simple heraldic charges, which in Western Europe are so typical of the earliest heraldry, are literally non-existent in Russian arms. Other charges, such as animals, were as a rule neither stylised nor portrayed in heraldic form, as is normal in Western Europe, but were shown in true form, sometimes even in natural surroundings, so that they look more like illustrations in a book on zoology than coats of arms.

In 1472 Ivan III (1462–1505) married Sophia, niece of the last ruler of the Eastern Roman Empire, which had fallen when the Turks conquered Constantinople (Byzantium) in 1453. Ivan III regarded himself as the heir to the Byzantine Empire and emphasised this by assuming the title of Czar (a derivative of the name and style Caesar), and taking the Byzantine double-headed eagle as his device. Yet an official description of the double-headed eagle as the arms of the Russian

Czars is not found until the close of the seventeenth century, when it was given new form and was proclaimed with the arms of thirty-three other realms and principalities which included the complete title of the Czars. This was done with the collaboration of an Imperial German herald who had been summoned by the Czar. At about the same time a register of Russian noble armorial bearings was compiled.

Peter the Great (1689–1725), who worked hard to introduce Western European ideas and institutions into his kingdom, took an active interest in heraldry. In 1722 he established a government department for heraldry directed by a 'master of heraldry', among whose duties was the creation of armorial bearings for all noble families that had none, and for all the officers of the army and navy. The 'vice-master of heraldry' was an Italian whose special task it was to design arms for Russian provinces and towns. He produced in all 137 such coats of arms, and the influence of French heraldry was very noticeable here. Heraldic matters became so important during this period that the Imperial Academy of Arts and Science invited a German professor in 1726 to give a lecture on heraldry.

There had from early times been many princely families in Russia, those who were the descendents of Rurik, who was the ruler of Novgorod 862–79 and was regarded as the founder of the Russian realm, and those whose ancestors were princes of Lithuania and Georgia or of Tartar origin. In 1707 Peter the Great made a complete innovation by raising his favourite Alexander Menschikov to the rank of titular prince. And this move, promotion to the aristocracy by grant of letters patent, was continued to an even greater extent by later rulers.

Under Peter the Great's daughter Elizabeth (1741–61) the Office of Heraldry issued 200 patents of nobility, some of them to the soldiers who had helped her to power (see p. 157), and up to 1797 patents of nobility giving a right to armorial bearings were granted to 355 persons with no previous title, as well as to thirty-seven barons and counts.

Coats of arms were as a rule depicted on a shield known as 'French' (p. 153). People newly raised to the aristocracy bore a helmet with raised visor in profile (Fig. 812), the old nobility a barred helmet affronty, sometimes with a coronet (Figs 274 and 815). There were other coronets for barons (Fig. 813) and counts (Fig. 816). Princes had a right to a robe of estate and a prince's crown (Fig. 814). The arms of the ancient princely families were often shared by several branches with different names. The Princes Bariatinsky, who descended from Rurik and the old princes of Kiev, bore the arms of Kiev (see Fig. 824) together with those of Tchernigov (Fig. 814, also Figs 819 and 820).

232

The crest was often the main charge repeated, or three plumes might be used instead.

At the close of the eighteenth century the Emperor Paul (1796–1801) ordered the registration and proclamation of all Russian coats of arms borne by the aristocracy of the following six categories:

1. Nobility without title granted a patent of nobility by the Czar.

2. Noblesse d'épée, i.e. officers in the army and navy who had reached the rank of colonel and above.

3. Noblesse du cap, i.e. government officials who had reached a rank equivalent to colonel.

4. Foreign nobility who had become naturalised Russians.

5. Nobility already titled.

6. The old aristocracy, i.e. who were noble before 1685.

The first volume of this work appeared in 1798, but ten others that were planned were never printed, and in any case the work was incomplete. Before publication all armorial bearings were to be ratified by the Office of Heraldry and by the Czar himself, and since many of the families did not wish to submit to such an investigation they did nothing about it.

Similar works were planned for Russian Poland and the Ukraine. Here too the heraldic authorities demanded that a coat of arms should be ratified before it could be used or proclaimed, but this was never put into effect.

In 1780 all towns of a certain size which had no armorial bearings were ordered to assume one, and this again had to be confirmed by the Czar. Regional capitals as a rule used the same coat of arms as the region. The other towns used it as a chief (Fig. 67) in their own bearings. In 1857 this was changed to a canton (Fig. 71), and it was at this time, perhaps in imitation of Napoleonic heraldry (see Figs 487 and 489), that a system was introduced of mural crowns, gold, silver and red, with varying numbers of crenellations depending on the size of the population of the town and its administrative position, historical importance and so on. Moscow and St Petersburg were allowed to use the imperial crown (Figs 823 and 825) as well as the sceptre, the ribbon of the Order of St Andrew and other items.

During the same period it became customary to frame a civic coat of arms with a wreath of foliage or two green branches or ears of corn. It seems probable that the wreath of corn bound with ribbon in the arms of the Soviet Union (Fig. 833) – since copied by nearly all the communist states – is a continuation of this practice from Czarist times. The Russian Revolution of 1917 meant of course an end to all family arms.

National arms on the other hand continued to an even greater extent, although in a different form. The Czarist double-headed eagle disappeared and the hammer and sickle, symbol of the industrial and agricultural classes, took its place. In the arms of the Soviet Union the hammer and sickle are placed with the globe as background, and for the people of the world the red star of the Soviet heralded a new dawn (Fig. 833), a fact made comprehensible to all by its composition.

The position of civic heraldry today is not yet clear, but it certainly arouses interest. In recent years numerous publications with illustrations and information about the old civic arms from before 1917 have appeared in the Soviet Union, and it is quite possible that those which do not contain Czarist or religious devices, but are politically neutral, such as Figs 831 and 832, may be adopted once again.

The United States (pp. 159-61)

When the Europeans, especially those from Great Britain, Germany and Holland, emigrated to North America in the seventeenth and eighteenth centuries, they took their heraldic traditions with them, and these are still carried on today. Examples of such coats of arms can be seen in Maryland's flag, Fig. 837, a continuation of the arms of Lord Baltimore, whose son founded the colony in 1684, and the armorial bearings of the Washington and Franklin families (Figs 842 and 844). In the arms of Eisenhower, assumed by the president, the anvil is a play on the German word *Eisenhauer* (meaning 'blacksmith').

At this time an American heraldry developed too along the same lines, especially in the case of academic and similar institutions. Examples of this are shown in the arms of universities and colleges (Figs 843 and 847-49: see also Fig. 307). For Americans of British descent such arms were sometimes, and still are, officially registered by the heraldic authorities in Great Britain and Eire: the College of Arms in London, Lord Lyon King of Arms in Edinburgh and the Chief Herald of Ireland in Dublin, depending on which part of the British Isles they came from. Examples are found on pp. 67, 73 (Fig. 376) and 75. The arms of the film star Douglas Fairbanks junior (Fig. 845) are in a similar category; they depict the old world and the new joined by the band of friendship across the blue Atlantic.

As well as these traditional coats of arms there developed after the War of Independence in 1776 new forms of heraldry influenced by revolutionary symbols. Some of these were not far removed in their details from the old ones and this is particularly true of the arms of the republic itself (Fig. 836) and of the flags of various individual states

(Figs 839 and 840). Many of the new ones, especially seals designed during the nineteenth century, had nothing really to do with heraldry in the accepted sense of the word, but were rather what might be called pioneer and settler allegories. They are certainly of interest, but are in essence beyond the scope of this book and are therefore not dealt with.

There are various genealogical societies in the United States, many of which are devoted to heraldry as well. The oldest and best known is the New England Historic Genealogical Society, Newsbury Street 101, Boston, Mass.

Canada (p. 162)

In Canada there is a mixture of British, French and native Canadian heraldry of which the national coat of arms (Fig. 850) is a good example: the first quarter of the shield stands for England, the second for Scotland, the third for Ireland (Fig. 309), the fourth for France (Fig. 424) which is also represented by the banner held by the unicorn (see also the fleurs-de-lys in the arms of the province of Quebec, Fig. 852). Canada was French until about 1760.

The base with the maple leaves represents Canada itself. In the course of the nineteenth century the maple leaf became Canada's national symbol in contrast to the heraldic devices the country had inherited from its European immigrants, and in 1868 the two Canadian provinces, Ontario and Quebec, made the maple leaf a part of their arms (Figs 851 and 852). The maple leaf was added to the national coat of arms in 1921 and in 1965 it became the central motif in the new national flag of Canada.

In the reproduction of the arms of the province of British Columbia, Fig. 853, there should have been an antique or eastern crown (see Fig. 204) in the middle of the Union Jack forming the chief.

The address of The Heraldry Society of Canada (*La Société Héraldique du Canada*) is c/o Mr Norman A. Nunn, 900 Pinecrest Road, Ottawa 14, Ontario.

Mexico and South America (pp. 163–5)

As long as Mexico and South America belonged to Spain (and in the case of Brazil, to Portugal), the heraldry of these colonies was in the main an offshoot of that of the homelands. Charges of local origin were likely to be included – see the Indians' heads in Fig. 856 and the cacti in Fig. 857 – but this in no way changed the usual composition.

After the secessions at the beginning of the nineteenth century a new form of national and civic heraldry developed in certain respects. Some of the new states retained the shield of the old shape, while others did away with it (Figs 15, 854 and 858), but the devices themselves were all new: the Phrygian cap of liberty and the rising sun (Fig. 861), the laurel wreath (Figs 15 and 862), the clasped hands of brotherhood (Fig. 861), the cornucopia (Figs 860 and 862), stars and so on. The traditional heraldic beasts etc. were supplanted by native flora and fauna: the Queztal bird of Guatemala (Fig. 15), Brazil's wreath of coffee and tobacco leaves with the constellation of the Southern Cross in the centre (Fig. 858), Chile's hart and condor (Fig. 859), Peru's llama (Fig. 862) etc. In Mexico and the Small Central American states especially inspiration was also sought in Indian heraldry and symbolism (Fig. 854).

There are heraldic societies in Mexico and a number of other South American states.

Australia and South Africa (pp. 166–7)

British colonial heraldry developed in the nineteenth century particularly. An attempt was made to unite traditional forms of heraldry (as understood then) with devices that were characteristic of life and nature in the colonies. Measured by the yardstick of classical heraldry the result is as a rule not very successful, but it is typical of that period and interesting at times.

In the arms of Australia (Fig. 863) the second quarter, representing the state of Victoria, contains the Southern Cross (cf. Fig. 858); the fourth, for South Australia, a native type of shrike; the fifth, for Western Australia, a black swan. The supporters are a kangaroo and an emu.

As elsewhere in the world interest in heraldry is on the increase in Australia, the centre being The Heraldry Society of Australia, c/o Colonel A. G. Puttock, 19 Haverbrack Avenue, Malvern, S.E.4, Victoria.

In South Africa there is a mixture of Dutch and British heraldry. The Netherlands is exemplified for instance by the lion holding the fasces (Fig. 864), the latter symbolising strength through unity (compare the motto in Fig. 867). The flags that flank this latter coat of arms have a vertical green stripe added to the Netherlands flag. The tree in Fig. 864 is an orange tree, a play on the name of 'Oranje', which again is the Boer form of 'Oranien', the Dutch name for the Royal House of Orange. The wagon in the fourth quarter, which can also be seen in Fig. 867, is the covered ox-wagon used by the Boers in the Great Trek.

In Fig. 865 the chief contains the German eagle in memory of the fact that the province before the First World War was a German colony.

Interest in heraldry in the Republic of South Africa is so great that a few years ago the office of State Heraldist was established, with authority to design and register coats of arms both for state and civic institutions and for private individuals. There is a society, The Heraldry Society of Southern Africa (*Die Heraldiese Genootskap van Suidelike Afrika*), Postbox 4839, Cape Town.

The many African states that have become independent since the Second World War have to a great extent followed in the footsteps of formalised European heraldry. Many of them however have done away with the traditional shape of shield and have instead introduced African forms. Basutoland, which is now called Lesotho, has since 1966 borne its device, a crocodile, on a very distinctive native shield, a type seen at the top of Fig. 866. Other states (Kenya, Uganda, Tanzania, Botswana) bear their charges on an almond-shaped shield of the native type. This has been copied by the Evangelical Lutheran church of South Africa, among others (see Fig. 906).

Ecclesiastical Heraldry (pp. 168–76)

In the early days of heraldry, in the twelfth century, seals were already in use among bishops and other princes of the Church, and it was not long before they began to include coats of arms and other heraldic devices in them. The insignia of their ecclesiastical office, such as the bishop's mitre and the cross-staff and crosier, were frequently used. Eventually the prelate's hat was also used in the system devised by the Catholic Church to indicate the rank of the holder. The triple coronet called the tiara is the Pope's special crown (Figs 868, 875, 879 and 899). It was originally a tall, pointed, white hat combined with a coronet or open crown, which together stood for the Pope's authority as a secular prince. Pope Boniface VIII (1294–1303) added one more crown and Clement V (1305–14) yet another. At the back hang two ribbons ('infulae'), as a rule white with gold ornamentation (white and yellow are the papal colours), or yellow with red or purple decoration. The first pope to bear the tiara together with his family arms was John XXII (1316–34).

In the blazonry of the Catholic Church the bishop's mitre is used and borne by cardinals, patriarchs, archbishops, abbots and certain others. It is also used in the Anglican Church (Figs 237, 870 and 880) and in several other Protestant Churches (p. 176). Nowadays a bishop's mitre is usually reproduced in white or yellow with stones of various colours and with ribbons in corresponding colours.

The heraldic use of the flat prelate's hat of the Catholic Church with its cords and tassels can be traced back to the fourteenth century. For the next couple of centuries there were only two sorts: the red hat of the cardinal (Fig. 464) and the black of the papal protonotary. Gradually more were added and in 1833 the system now in force was laid down: Cardinals have red hats with fifteen tassels on each side (Fig. 883). Patriarchs, archbishops and bishops have green hats, patriarchs with fifteen tassels on each side (Fig. 890), archbishops with ten (Fig. 889), and bishops with six (Fig. 891). There are also a large number of black and purple hats with numbers of tassels down to one on each side, a selection of which is shown on pp. 174 and 175.

Other Catholic badges of office and rank are the crossed keys, the crosier and various types of cross-staff. Both crosiers and cross-staffs are also used in non-Catholic churches (p. 176).

The two crossed keys, 'St Peter's keys', are first and foremost the device of the Pope. Together with the tiara they make up the arms of the Vatican City and are also included in the arms of a large number of existing or former papal possessions (for example in the civic arms of Naestvaed in Denmark, which in the Middle Ages came within the jurisdiction of the local monastery of St Peter). Nowadays one of the keys is usually gold and the other silver, tied with a red cord. Together with another item of papal insignia, an object resembling an umbrella and called an *ombrellino*, they are borne by families who have had a member on the papal throne, and also by certain institutions.

The crosier or shepherd's crook in gold is borne by bishops and abbots (Figs 887 and 893), by priors, usually in silver – sometimes in a different shape. On the crosier of an abbot or prior there is usually a piece of silk, a 'sudarium' (Fig. 877) or napkin, intended to soak up the dampness of the hand. When bishops do not bear a sudarium it is because their vestments include ceremonial gloves.

The cross-staff is borne by bishops (Fig. 891): archbishops also have it, but with the arms of the cross doubled. The colour is usually gold.

A pallium is a broad pall worn over both shoulders. It is the symbol of office for functioning archbishops (as compared with titular archbishops) and in more recent heraldry is sometimes shown as an adjunct to the coat of arms (Fig. 888). In England a pallium is included in the arms of the province of Canterbury (see Fig. 880).

BIBLIOGRAPHY AND ACKNOWLEDGMENTS

In addition to the many dictionaries and historical works in general that I have consulted in the preparation of this book I would like to express my appreciation to the authors, illustrators and publishers of the heraldic and other publications which I have referred to more directly (note: the English language editor has made a number of additions to the author's list, principally in the section relating to Great Britain):

General

D. L. Galbreath, *Manuel du Blason* (Lausanne, 1942); German edition, *Handbüchlein der Heraldik* (1948).

Boutell's Heraldry, revised edn., J. P. Brooke-Little (London and New York, 1978).

H. G. Ströhl, *Heraldischer Atlas* (Stuttgart, 1899).

Iain Moncreiffe and Don Pottinger, *Simple Heraldry Cheerfully Illustrated* (London, 1953, and later editions).

Baron Stalins, *Vocabulaire-Atlas Heraldique* (Paris, 1952).

Preben Kannik, *Alverdens flag i farver* (Copenhagen, 1956); 2nd edn. ed. C. F. Pedersen (Copenhagen, 1970); Eng. Lang. edn., *The International Flag Book in Colour*, ed. J. H. B. Bedells (London, 1971).

C. A. von Volborth, *Little Manual of Heraldry* (Torrance, California, 1966).

Augustan Society Roll of Arms, 1967/8, illustr. C. A. von Volborth (Torrance, California, 1968).

Jiři Louda, *European Civic Coats of Arms* (London, 1966).

Edward Francis, Lord Twining, *European Regalia* (London, 1967).

Paul Lacroix, *Science and Literature in the Middle Ages and the Renaissance* (New York, 1964).

Great Britain

Boutell's Heraldry, revised edn., J. P. Brooke-Little (London and New York, 1978).

Geoffrey Briggs, *Civic and Corporate Heraldry* (London, 1971).

Burke's General Armory (London, 1884 edn., and later impressions).

A. C. Fox-Davies, *A Complete Guide to Heraldry*, revised edn., J. P. Brooke-Little (London, 1969).

Sir W. H. St. J. Hope, *A Grammar of English Heraldry*, revised edn.,
A. R. Wagner (1953).

A. R. Wagner, *Historic Heraldry of Britain* (1939 and later impressions).

Oswald Barron, 'Heraldry', *Encyclopaedia Britannica*, 11th edn. (1910/11).

A. R. Wagner, 'Heraldry', *Chambers's Encyclopaedia* (1966 edn.).

Heather Child, *Heraldic Design* (London, 1965, and later impressions).

G. W. Fairbairn, *A Book of Crests*, 4th edn., 2 vols (London, 1905).

J. W. Papworth, *Ordinary of British Armorials*, ed. A. W. Morant (London,
1874, and leter impressions).

J. H. Parker, *A Glossary of Terms used in British Heraldry* (1847 and later
editions).

C. W. Scott-Giles, *The Romance of Heraldry*, 4th edn. (1957).

C. W. Scott-Giles, *Shakespeare's Heraldry* (1950, new impression 1971).

G. D. Squibb, *The Law of Arms in England*, revised edn. (London, 1967).

A. R. Wagner, *A Catalogue of English Mediaeval Rolls of Arms* (London,
1950).

A. R. Wagner, *Heralds and Heraldry in the Middle Ages*, 2nd edn. (Oxford,
1956, and later impressions).

Sir Anthony Wagner, *Heralds of England* (London, 1967).

C. W. Scott-Giles, *Civic Heraldry of England and Wales*, 2nd edn. (1953).

Scotland

Sir Thomas Innes of Learney, *Scots Heraldry* (Edinburgh, 1934; 2nd
edn., 1956, and later impressions).

*The Scottish Tartans with Historical Sketches of the Clans and Families of
Scotland*, revised edn., Sir Thomas Innes of Learney (Edinburgh, 1963).

Iain Moncreiffe and Don Pottinger, *Simple Heraldry Cheerfully Illustrated*
(London, 1953, and later editions).

C. R. MacKinnon of Dunakin, *Scotland's Heraldry* (Glasgow, 1962).

The Netherlands

C. Pama, *Handboek der Wapenkunde* (1961).

Kl. Sierksma, *De gemeentewapens van Nederland* (Utrecht, 1960).

Belgium

Baron de Ryckman de Betz, *Armorial Général de la Noblesse Belge* (Liège,
1957).

France

Rémi Mathieu, *Le Système Héraldique Français* (Paris, 1946).

Napoleonic
Henry Simon, *Armorial Général de l'Empire Francais* (Paris, 1812, and later editions).
Germany
Hugo Gerard Ströhl, *Deutsche Wappenrolle* (Stuttgart, 1897).
A. M. Hildebrandt, *Wappenfibel* (Frankfurt am Main, 1909, and later editions).
R. G. Stillfried, *Die Attribute des Neuen Deutschen Reiches* (Berlin, 1872).
Der Deutsche Herold (periodical, 1873, current).
Otto Hupp, *Deutsche Ortswappen* (Vol. 1, Bremen, 1913, and later volumes).
Ottfried Neubecker, *Von Friedrich dem Grossen bis Hindenburg, 265 ruhmreiche deutsche Wappen* (series of cigarette cards, 1934).
Die Minnesinger in Bildern der Manessischen Handschrift (Leipzig, c. 1933).
Klemens Stadler, *Deutsche Wappen. Bundesrepublik Deutschland* (Vol. 1, Bremen, 1964, and later volumes).
Deutsches Geschlechterbuch (Vol. 1, 1889, and later volumes).
Genealogisches Handbuch des Adels (Vol. 1, 1942, and later volumes).
S. Gutmann, *Ärzte- und Apothekerwappen* (Baden-Baden, 1962).

Austria
Franz Gall, *Österreich und seine Wappen* (Vienna, 1968).

Switzerland
D. L. Galbreath, *Manuel du Blason* (Lausanne, 1942); German edn., *Handbüchlein der Heraldik* (1948).
H. R. von Fels, *Wappenbuch der Stadt St. Gallen* (1952).

Portugal
F. P. de Almeida Langhans, *Heráldica, ciência de temas vivos* (Lisbon, 1966).
Jaime Lopes Dias, *Brasão da cidade de Lisboa* (Lisbon, 1968).
Roger F. Pye, 'Names, Arms and Cadency in Portugal', *The Coat of Arms,* Vol. 8, No. 62 (London, 1965).

Spain
Vicente de Cadenas y Vicent, *Diccionario Heráldico* (Madrid, 1954).
Alberto y Arturo Garcia Carraffa, *Ciencia heráldica o del blasón* (Madrid, 1957).
Julio de Atienza, *Nobiliario español* (Madrid, 1954).
Estado Mayor Central del Ejército, *Tratado de heráldica militar* (Madrid, 1959).

241

Italy

Robert Gayre of Gayre and Nigg, 'The Administration of Heraldry in Republican Italy', *The Coat of Arms*, Vol. 5, No. 35 (London, 1958). *Bollettino Ufficiale del Corpo della Nobiltà Italiana* (Vol. 1, 1958).

Denmark

Sven Tito Achen, 'Danske kommunevåbener', in Hvem-Hvad-Hvor ('Who-What-Where') (2nd edn.) 1968, (Copenhagen, 1967); also as an offprint.

Norway

Hans A. K. T. Cappelen, *Norske slektsvåpen* (Oslo, 1969).

Sweden

C. A. Klingspor, *Sveriges ridderskaps och adels vapenbok* (1890).
Uno Lindgren, *Heraldik i svenska författningar* (Lund, 1951).
Arvid Berghman, *Heraldisk bilderbok*, with illustrations by Sven Sköld (Stockholm, 1951).
N. L. Rasmusson, 'Rikets vapen', and Svante Svardstrom, 'Sveriges flagga', in *Rikets vapen och flagga* (Stockholm, 1960).
Skandinavisk vapenrulla, ed. Jan Raneke and Christer Bökwall (Vol. 1, Malmö, 1963, and later volumes).
C. G. U. Scheffer, *Svensk vapenbok för landskap, län och städer* (Stockholm, 1967).

Poland

S. Konarski, *Armorial de la noblesse polonaise titrée*, with drawings by, among others, Rober Louis (Paris, 1958).
M. Gumowski, *Herby miast polskich* (Warsaw, 1960).
Adam Heymowski, 'Polish Arms in Medieval Armorials', *The Coat of Arms*, Vol. 8, No. 58 (London, 1964).

Russia

Armorial Général de Russie, Vols. 1-7 (St. Petersburg, 1798–1836).
V. K. Lukomsky and Baron N. A. Tiepold, *Russkaya Heraldika* (St Petersburg, 1915).

The United States

America Heraldica, ed. E. de V. Vermont (New York, 1886).
The Heraldic Journal, No. 15 (1866).
Hubert Allcock, *Heraldic Design* (New York, 1962).
George Earlie Shankle, *State Names, Flags, Seals, Songs, Birds, Flowers*

and Other Symbols (New York, 1941).
The Arms of Yale University and its Colleges at New Haven (1963).

South Africa
C. Pama, *Lions and Virgins. Heraldic State Symbols, Coats-of-Arms, Flags, Seals and Other Symbols of Authority in South Africa 1487–1962* (Cape Town, 1965).

Ecclesiastical Heraldry
Mgr Bruno Bernard Heim, *Wappenbrauch und Wappenrecht in der Kirche* (Olten, Switzerland, 1947); French edition, *Coutumes et droit héraldiques de l'Eglise* (Paris, 1949).

In conclusion I would like to emphasise that in spite of extensive study I would not have found it possible to gather all the information given in the present book if specialists in the subject, each an expert in his field, had not generously responded to my requests and given me and my book the benefit of their knowledge. Among them I must mention the following: Edward J. B. Irving (Scottish heraldry); John Gerard Slevin, A.I.H. (i.e. member of the *Académie Internationale d'Heraldique*) (Irish heraldry); O. Schutte (Netherlands heraldry); Baron Hervé Pinoteau, A.I.H. (French heraldry); Franz Gall, A.I.H. (Austrian heraldry); George Bislin and Gottfried Zengin (Swiss heraldry); Endre de Tamaska de Baranch and Szabolcs de Vajay, A.I.H. (Hungarian heraldry); F. P. de Almeida Langhans and Marc Rangel de Algeciras (Portuguese heraldry); Faustino Menendez Pidal de Navascues, A.I.H. (Spanish heraldry); Baron A. Monti della Corte (Italian heraldry); Ole Rostock and Sven Tito Achen, A.I.H. (Danish heraldry); Hans A. K. T. Cappelen (Norwegian heraldry); Leif Påhlsson, Baron Christopher von Warnstedt, Hans Schlyter, A.I.H., Brother Bengt Olof Kälde and Gunnar Scheffer, A.I.H. (Swedish heraldry); Gustaf von Numers, A.I.H. (Finnish heraldry); Alexander von Kempski Rakoszyn and Adam Heymowski, A.I.H. (Polish heraldry); N. Djounkovsky (Russian heraldry); Rodney E. Hartwell (North American heraldry and heraldry in general); Luis León de la Barra (Mexican heraldry); Cornelius Pama, A.I.H. (South African and Dutch heraldry); and Mgr Bruno Bernhard Heim, A.I.H. (Ecclesiastical heraldry). I would like to thank all these expert heraldists for their assistance, valuable advice and constructive criticism. Errors, which

243

the book may contain in spite of every care, are entirely the responsibility of the author, unless they have occurred as a result of alterations to his original text.

Carl Alexander von Volborth, A.I.H.

INDEX OF ARMS AND DEVICES
ILLUSTRATED

References are to figure numbers except where otherwise stated.